THE CALL TO BE HUMAN

THE CALL TO BE HUMAN
Making Sense of Morality

Vincent MacNamara

VERITAS

Published 2010 by
Veritas Publications
7–8 Lower Abbey Street
Dublin 1
Ireland

publications@veritas.ie
www.veritas.ie

ISBN 978-1-84730-213-7

10 9 8 7 6 5 4 3 2

A catalogue record for this book is available from the British
Library.

Designed by Lir Mac Cárthaigh
Printed in Ireland by ColourBooks Ltd., Dublin

*Veritas books are printed on paper made from the wood pulp of
managed forests. For every tree felled, at least one tree is
planted, thereby renewing natural resources.*

PREFACE

Twenty years ago I wrote a book called *The Truth in Love: Reflections on Christian Morality*. It was well received and I hope that it may have done some good. Eventually it went out of print. I have had many requests to reprint it over the years. I did not do so, because I knew that I could not be satisfied without some rewriting. I now offer *The Call To Be Human: Making Sense of Morality*, which I consider to be a new book, although it covers the same general area of fundamental Christian morality and borrows slightly from the earlier work. My hope is that it will give confidence to people generally to engage in moral discussion in Church and State. I have tried, as far as possible, to avoid technical discussion and terminology. Those who work in the field of morality will see that I have taken shortcuts and will recognise the need for qualification and development. They will also know that, as in all work of this kind, I am standing on the shoulders of many who have made much more significant contributions to moral science. I hope that this book will prompt readers to a deeper study of the area.

A number of good friends have encouraged me with this project, have read the text and have made helpful suggestions. I thank especially Eamonn Bredin, Bairbre and Máirtín de Búrca, Áilín Doyle, Patrick Hannon and Suzanne Mulligan. My best thanks are also due to Caitríona Clarke of Veritas for her painstaking editorial work.

ACKNOWLEDGEMENTS

'My Mother's Sister' by C. Day Lewis, taken from *The Oxford Book of Twentieth Century Verse* (Philip Larkin, ed.), Oxford, Oxford University Press, 1973, 356.

'Docker' by Seamus Heaney, taken from *Death of a Naturalist*, London, Faber and Faber, 1991, 28.

'The Garden of Love' by William Blake, taken from *The Poems of William Blake* (W.B. Yeats, ed.), London, Routledge and Kegan Paul, 1979, 76.

'Next Please' by Philip Larkin, taken from *Collected Poems*, Victoria/London, Marvell Press/Faber and Faber, 2003, 50.

'Experimental Animals' by Denis O'Driscoll, taken from *New and Selected Poems*, London, Anvil, 2004, 83.

'Ancient Lights' by Austin Clarke, taken from *Collected Poems* (R. Dardis Clarke, ed.), Manchester, Carcanet, 199; used with permission, R. Dardis Clarke, 17 Oscar Square, Dublin 8.

'Sonnet on Hearing the *Dies Irae* Sung in the Sistine Chapel' by Oscar Wilde, taken from *Complete Poetry of Oscar Wilde*, Oxford, Oxford World Classics, 2009, 24.

'A Disused Shed in Co. Wexford' by Derek Mahon, taken from *Collected Poems*, Oldcastle, Gallery Press, 1999, 89.

'For Anne Gregory' by W.B. Yeats, taken from *Collected Poems of W.B. Yeats*, London, Macmillan and Co., 1958.

'Last Court' by John Montague, taken from John McDonagh, *A Fine Statement: An Irish Poet's Anthology*, Dublin, Poolbeg Press, 2008, 205.

'Ars Poetica?' by Czesław Miłosz, taken from *Collected Poems, 1931–2001*, London, Penguin, 2001, 240.

'St Kevin and the Blackbird' by Seamus Heaney, taken from *Opened Ground*, London, Faber and Faber, 1998, 410.

'In memory of Sigmund Freud' by W.H. Auden, taken from *Collected Poems* (Edward Mendelson, ed.), London, Faber and Faber, 1979, 91.

Quotations from the Second Vatican Council are from Austin Flannery, O.P. (ed.), *Vatican Council II: Constitutions, Decrees, Declarations*, New York/Dublin, Costello Publishing Co./Dominican Publications, 1996.

Scripture quotations are taken from *The New English Bible*, Oxford–Cambridge, 1970.

CONTENTS

CHAPTER 1
Approaching Morality

I think we can dive right into the subject. Morality is not a foreign country. We all know a lot about it. It constantly surfaces in our conversations. People argue about inequalities in our health or educational system, about same-sex marriage, about war, about the treatment of immigrants, about the bonuses of bankers, about the waste of public money, about abortion, about the welfare of children, about the failure of bishops. They write letters to the papers. They demonstrate, they sign petitions. They don't always use the traditional moral language of right and wrong. They say that certain pieces of conduct or ways of behaving or institutions are outrageous or unacceptable or inhuman or indefensible. Or, on the other hand, they claim that they have a moral right to certain kinds of treatment or an entitlement to certain benefits.

We are right to talk and argue about such things. It is because we have a sense of the moral dimension of life that we do so. It is to such that we are appealing. After all, why should anyone listen to you or engage with you or take you seriously when you talk or write about rights or obligations or injustice or unfairness? We certainly expect them to listen; we think we are justified. There is some kind of unspoken common ground on which we depend, to which we can appeal. It is an acknowledgment of the moral point of view. It seems to be true that we cannot describe how life presents itself to us, we cannot have a society, without recourse to some of the language of 'right' 'wrong', 'good', 'bad', 'duty', 'obligation', 'ought', 'praise', 'blame', as well as much moral language of a softer kind – 'unacceptable', 'not the decent thing'.

So it seems to be part of our humanness, of our intelligence, to take this for granted. We may have trouble nailing it down. We may be only able to assert it, to say that we know that there are things that are right and wrong but not go much further in the way of explaining it, or accounting for it, or spelling out its implications. But we do seem to regard it as entirely natural to accept it. So we know a great deal and that is the best place to begin any discussion of morality – with ourselves and our spontaneous ideas and judgments, with what we do and expect. I think you would agree that, when we make moral statements, we do not think that we are merely expressing our tastes: they are not in the same category as statements such as I like science fiction, or Indian cinema, or spaghetti bolognese, or the

Connemara landscape, and don't like cucumber or modern architecture. It is perfectly alright for you to like one thing and for me to like another. Such things do not greatly matter; there is no right and wrong or true and false about them. But there are areas of life in which it matters a great deal what we value and do – issues of a person's right to life, of justice, of respect, of cruelty, of hunger, of political corruption, of banking scandals, of child abuse, i.e. moral issues. We are not prepared to say that in making statements about such matters we are merely expressing a subjective point of view and that it is perfectly fine for someone else to hold and act on the opposite point of view.

A Truth for Living

No, we believe that there is what we might call an objectivity about such statements. You would not blame someone for not liking cucumber or tomato but you would blame them for espousing cruelty or torture or the abuse of children, or being callous about people dying of hunger. We believe that there is a truth to be discovered here, a truth for living that is as rigorous as truth in any other area, and that the judgments we are making are somehow founded in the natures and relations of things. We would expect to be able to give reasons of some kind for our positions, to justify them. Or, at least, we feel that they are justifiable, that someone who was good at understanding the human situation and was articulate could demonstrate the reasonableness of them. I don't think you would settle for saying 'well, it was fine if they felt that cruelty or torture or abuse was OK'? I don't think so – you would have to deal with Hitler and Mao and Pol Pot and many of the great crimes of history if you followed that line. There is something here that has a validity, that is undeniable, whatever people think.

Can we develop this a bit more? We use the words 'wrong' or 'right', but if you were challenged to say what you mean by them, what would you say? What does it mean to you to say that something is 'wrong'? Why do we feel justified in appealing to it or expecting others to take it seriously? Or if someone says to you, 'you cannot do that, it is wrong', where does the 'cannot' come from? I don't mean now what *kinds* of acts are wrong, but what do you mean by saying that *anything* is wrong? Does it mean for you, for example, that it is forbidden by God or forbidden by the ten commandments – you know how often you have heard people condemn a crime by saying that it is 'a crime against the sacred and inviolable law of God'. That may have its place. There was a time when most people would give that answer, but less and less people would give that answer today. (And they'd be right, but more about that in chapter five.)

I suspect that people today would explain what they mean by appealing to such rock-bottom notions as harm, or fairness, or impartiality, or justice, or respect for self and others, or by talk about rights, or by concern for a just society. Or talk about what kind of life is fitting or appropriate for human beings. These are related ideas. What they all imply is that you are going beyond mere assertion. You are not saying arrogantly, 'Well, it is wrong and that is the end of it', or 'it is wrong because my church says so', or 'it is wrong because that is what I feel about it', or 'it is wrong because it is wrong'. You are getting into a deeper question, the 'why' question – 'why do I say this is wrong?' You are reaching back beyond mere assertion to something more fundamental in human life. You are trying to give reasons that have to do with your sense – and you hope everyone else's sense – of what it means to be a human being. So you would be pushing things back a bit and saying that it is wrong *because* – because it is harmful, or discriminatory, or lacking in respect, or cruel, or is bad for society, or denies another's rights, or makes no human sense, or whatever. And you would expect people to understand that and acknowledge it – at least to understand what you are getting at. This is our moral experience.

So we seem to have a vision, a sense of what being human in the world involves. And more precisely what being human in the world with others involves. We are naturally social animals and the actions that we judge to be naturally right and just are not right and just in some abstract universe but in human society, in the interface with others. So morality begins with what is – with our sense of what it means to be a human being with others in society, and not an orangutan or a cow. It is founded on that. There is some notion here of what is a characteristically human life, a worthwhile life, or a fulfilled life, or, in a deep and considered sense of that word, a happy life. There is involved a sensitivity to the reality of being a human being, to its basic desires or dynamic, some sense of potential, of human evolution.

Human Needs

Well, that's where our morality begins. But let us pursue it a bit further. When we look at our spontaneous moral statements or concerns – justice for all, honesty in government, an end to discrimination etc. – we can see that they are about what human beings need for their well-being. What that involves is arrived at by our experience of living, our common experience of human needs and interests. Morality is not a matter of arcane laws. It is an understanding of what is good or fulfilling or growth-making for people – and that is the only justification any society or institution or church can have for promoting it. We all have ideas about that, and so we should. Your mother might tell you that vegetables are good for you, or fresh air, or exercise – and that too much drink is bad for you and that drugs will ruin your life. It is that kind of thing. The terms 'right' and 'good' are often used loosely – and often interchangeably – for the moral life. Strictly, however, 'good' is factual: it refers to what will bring about our flourishing or wholeness – understanding, for example, the importance to us of security, friendship, freedom, self-esteem, privacy, sex, leisure, and so on. 'Right' more strictly refers to what to do; it rests on our human sense that what is truly 'good' for us is to be followed, that it is the only thing that makes sense.

If you were to ask people around you what humans need for a fulfilled life, you would probably get a fair amount of agreement. Off the top of their heads they might mention all sorts of trivial things – because we are not always wise. But if you could sit them down and have them reflect, or meet them in decisive moments, it might be different. 'If only I could get rid of the pain', 'if only we had a place to live', 'if only my husband would give up the drink', 'if only my child would give up drugs', 'if only I had peace of mind', 'if only I had a friend, someone to talk to', 'if only I didn't feel so depressed about myself', 'if only we had peace and freedom in our country' – you might hear that kind of thing. Such situations drive us back to what is vital for us. If, then, we have an awareness of the needs of our human nature, we can know the direction of moral life, we can have some idea of how we ought to live together. It will be in the direction of what will enable our needs to be met – or what kind of society will enable it. A society that is fair, that protects the young and the vulnerable, that cares for the less fortunate, that nourishes us educationally and culturally, that makes it possible for us to make a living, to live in peace and security, to participate politically, to be free to pursue our convictions, and so on. These are things we consider worthwhile: they are worth pursuing and hoping for.

They are values for us. It is relatively easy to have this general sense of the direction of satisfactory living. It is much more difficult to settle on the more precise demands and that is where much of the argument occurs. (As in most matters, some are better at this than others: they have a better sense of the needs and possibilities of the human person. They have grown in wisdom. And some are simply good at being human.) But we'll come to that in chapters four, ten and eleven.

A Fact of History

This kind of concern for how we need to live together is an abiding fact in our history and literature. In all cultures and at all times, men and women have had their moral codes. They may differ about what is right and wrong. They may differ about how they arrive at their conclusions. They may have only analogous notions of morality. It may sometimes be difficult to disentangle it from other kinds of rules in their society, for example, religious or ritual rules, or conventions of etiquette. But they have had no doubt that some kinds of act, purpose and intention are right and the opposite wrong – some kinds of conduct to be accepted or praised, the opposite to be frowned upon and blamed, and perhaps not tolerated in society. The details of their positions on life, justice, fairness, community, sexuality, may differ from culture to culture and from age to age – we will see why later, and see problems to which this gives rise. But it is striking that there is enough broad agreement among different cultures and traditions to permit a document like the UN Declaration of Human Rights to lay out for all peoples what kind of conduct is acceptable, and how all human beings should be treated in matters of justice, life and so on. That document stands as a beacon against all forms of arbitrariness and abuse. It is saying that life cannot be arbitrarily lived, any old way we like, and that people cannot be arbitrarily treated. Why? Because of a deep conviction, which it trusts is shared by all peoples, that 'all human beings are born free and equal in dignity and rights'. It rests on this conviction of the inviolable quality of humans and their needs. It recognises that this is something deeper than and prior to agreements between governments. This acknowledgment by our intelligence, or soul, or humanness, is the lynchpin of society.

The Declaration is in the line of great classic statements down through the ages. We have it in philosophical and religious texts. But it is a constant also in the world's great literature – the struggle of right and wrong, of goodness and badness in living. But we don't need to go back through the ages: we have recent examples. How come we can agree to have international courts of justice and rights? To what do they appeal? Strikingly, when they arraign those who are charged with war crimes, even when they were committed under the duress of state directives, the courts have recourse to the language of 'crimes against humanity'. Their judgments are based on the authority of a moral order that the human spirit recognises as overriding all other authority. It points to the inner nature and source of morality. To its inescapable humanness. To the fact that it is difficult to be an intelligent human being and deny it.

There are anomalies, of course. Moral awareness can be dimmed and can fade. If we are morally careless over time, then the demand of our moral being loses its sharpness. We can silence remorse for our wrongdoing. That happens. What is more disturbing is to find someone who never had any moral sense, for whom the moral dimension of life is a complete blank, someone who sees nothing wrong in any of the moral evils that revolt the generality. One, who not merely approves or enjoys or condones wrongdoing, but cannot grasp what conceivable objection anyone could have to, let us suppose, torturing people for fun. Such a one is, sadly, an emotional cripple who does not have the equipment for a full human life. Acceptance of some fundamental notion of morality enters into our conception of a normal human being.

In doing morality, then, we are concerning ourselves with one of the great questions of life: what does it mean to be a human being, a person; how is one to live? It is a question that arises spontaneously for us and that has troubled humankind from the beginning. It is not something that we make but rather something that we find and to which our human nature tells us we must attend. Neither is it something that we can easily manipulate; the normal person feels the pinch of remorse if it is ignored; in this sense it is something greater than ourselves. Some speak about it as having a sacred character – so, for example, you hear talk about the sacred character of human life. I take that to mean that it is perceived and experienced as something of the deepest importance and dignity, something overriding other considerations, something which we must respect or pay the price of knowing that we have not been true to ourselves, that we have denied our soul, that we have failed in our deepest core. Morality is not the servant of our desires and interests, but their judge. We cannot commandeer it into our service.

A Search
We might think of the moral codes of the world as the result of this engagement of the human race from the beginning. It is a continuing, delicate and fragile search. Any society can get it wrong. Every society will probably agree that past conclusions were mistaken or need to be modified. Many societies will not only fine-tune what they received from earlier generations. They will change the weight and importance they give to one piece of morality or immorality over another. Think of the well-worn examples of slavery or of the status of women – Plato, Aristotle and St Paul would probably have told you that it was part of the natural law that some are born slaves and some free or that women are inferior to men. Think, too, of how our own societies have developed – its relatively recent acknowledgment of our

moral obligation to people with a disability, travellers, immigrants, those born out of wedlock, people in second relationships, those facing repossession of their homes. Think of issues like capital punishment, pre-marital sex, international trade, equal pay, the environment. At the very least there has been a change of emphasis. One could think of the whole of humanity slowly and painfully trying to work out over the ages what it means to live satisfactorily together. In a sense it is true to say that we make our morality. At least we discover it. But 'discovery' here is not like finding something ready-made. We have to work at it, to figure out what is best for humanity. And that calls for sensitivity.

Who is to say, people often ask. Who is to say what is right and wrong? Who is to decide whether a particular position or movement is an instance of greater moral insight, or the opposite – let's say IVF, or assisted suicide, or democracy, or liberal capitalism? Some find it difficult to accept that moral wisdom depends on our fallible minds. But that is how it is. It is no more likely that we will have certainty here than about anything else that is important – psychology, philosophy, medicine. Even the much lauded science is now seen as a matter of probabilities or hypotheses. And we are largely ignorant of important issues of faith: we know so little about God, or about life after death. If we do not know the answers to many of the problems in these areas, why should we expect to know all about morality? You could consult your tradition or your elders. You would be foolish to ignore that. But how do or did they know? Together, we have to do the best we can. There is nobody to go to, at least nobody except our fellow human beings. There is only the age-old search of humankind to listen to its deepest inspirations. Aristotle would have told you to go to the wise person, and that is helpful advice, if you could recognise one!

We see divisions daily between those who are happy to see society in this state of continuing search and discovery – in the area of morals as in every other area – and those who see morality as settled and handed down, perhaps by God, and given to institutions like the church to defend. For the second group, questions about morality are non-questions: all has been determined. Their fear is that questioning will lead to carelessness, that a precious heritage will be lost, and that the structure of church and society will be weakened. Respect for one's heritage is commendable. But morality is more fundamental than that: there is room for and need for thoughtful questioning. The chasm between the two approaches makes dialogue difficult and is often the source of disagreement on particular issues.

It is not surprising that we disagree about what is right and wrong, about who is the good human being. We are making value-judgments. We disagree about more tangible things. Not everyone will agree on what is a good table or lawnmower or poem. About such things as the length of a table or poem we cannot escape agreement – just get your measuring-tape or count the lines. That's easy. But with a 'good table' we are in a different category. That requires some understanding on what tables are *for*, what they are meant to do. Still less will they agree on what is to count as a good cook or cabinet-maker or gardener, although that might be possible – again, what are they *for*, what are they meant to do or produce? And as for agreement on a good poem or painting! About a good man or woman we have even greater problems. That has to do not with a person's skills – cooking, cabinet-making, gardening – which might be in some way measurable. It seems to mean 'good at being human' and that is a bit intangible. What are human beings *for*? What are they meant to be – if one can give sense to that expression? Who is the ideal human being? That is difficult. The meaning of life is much more difficult to discern than the meaning of a table or lawnmower or gardener. We do, however, have some basic sense of it and we should trust it.

We may rejoice in our gift of a moral sense and in its enduring presence in human society. It gives hope to us all. But that is only half the story. Many of us feel burdened by it: it is an uncomfortable friend; we can resent its insistence in our lives. It makes demands on us. Those of us who belong to a church sometimes see it as imposed on us 'from outside', as something that we have had no say in, and may feel that we have been saddled with a strict and damaging version of it. So that it might be important to see morality as something arising within ourselves, as our own doing, as the call of our deepest and best self. As something that we all have a right to discuss. We need to take ownership of it. This book is meant to be an encouragement to do so. If our experience of it has been confined and dispiriting, if our picture of it has been largely negative, we have a task to lift morality out of its narrowness and give it its true space. It is good to remember that it is the gift of our moral sense that drives us to fight against apartheid, to rage at the abuse of children, to run marathons for good causes, to build houses in the developing world, to work with Meals on Wheels, to provide shelter for Aids victims, to be concerned about human trafficking, to visit children's hospitals, and so on. It invites us to build a better world. There is a need for all of us to be ever questioning and wondering about our lives together. We might see ourselves on a journey to discover what our humanness is saying to us, what vision it is holding out to us, what is important and what not.

CHAPTER 2
The Moral Journey

I say that morality is a matter of humanness. It is true that some deny it or ignore it, some in a frighteningly destructive way – think of Auschwitz, or the Gulag, or My Lai, or Rwanda, or Gaza, or Srebrenica, or Guantanamo. For whatever reason, some become so crassly uncaring or so deaf that there seems no point in putting moral considerations to them. You would have to say about them that they are denying their human intelligence. Happily, most of us have a basic moral sense quite instinctively. But we have problems too: we all recognise that having a moral awareness is one thing and living up to it is another. We know about the gap. There are times when moral considerations have no bite for us. So it is well to recognise that our moral awareness is a sensitive plant. It can be nurtured and, if it is, it grows into richer and fuller life. What this chapter says is that such genuine growth hinges on listening to our humanness.

We can grow in moral sensitivity and consciousness – or we can regress. We know only too well the stuff that seduces us – the inordinate lure of power or wealth or pleasure, the fears, jealousies, envies, the things that in the moment are desirable or possess us. God help us, we are plagued with that sort of stuff and we can be depressed. But let us reflect too on the goodness in us. There are significant moments and movements that we tend to ignore, because they are below the surface of the everyday. It is important to acknowledge them, to do ourselves justice, to be open to a more adequate sense of ourselves. All of our life is not spent in pleasuring and competing and winning, or wallowing in hurts and resentments. We are, aren't we, sometimes moved, even to tears, by beauty and innocence and happiness, by the strangeness and the mystery of things. We have a natural admiration for goodness and truth. We appreciate love and trust. We are restless for peace and tranquillity. We have experiences of closeness and intimacy that make us feel the wonder of being human. The point is that there is depth to us as persons. We have experiences which nourish our soul and delight our spirit. They do not come easily in our modern, narrowly technological culture with its flattening of our language to the measurable and instrumental. It may be that we are more open to the soul and to goodness through poetry, liturgy and art than through rational investigation or speculation. Which is why we need our poets and painters and musicians and spiritual guides, with their images and symbols, to awaken us to the ecstasy and the heartbreak of being human. To keep alive in us our rich desires and possibilities. To keep us from selling ourselves short as human beings. To keep us from missing the point.[1]

You might not regard such areas as specifically moral. But our moral sense, I would argue, is part of this dimension. It is part of the beauty and the mystery of being a person. It is about not settling for miserable and paltry satisfactions. Not allowing ourselves to be fobbed off by unworthy desires of power or fame, or jealousy, or revenge. Not being imprisoned in the narrow interests of our own ambitions and pleasures, deaf to the needs and sufferings of our world. If we give ourselves credit, we recognise that there are in us also what are more precisely moral moments, moments of goodness and love and generosity and sympathy. We

---

1.'Art makes places and opens spaces for reflection, it is a defence against materialism and against pseudo-scientific attitudes to life ... The art object conveys, in the most accessible and for many the only available form, the idea of a transcendent perfection ... It renders innocent and transforms into truthful vision our baser energies connected with power, curiosity, envy and sex.' Iris Murdoch, 'Conceptions of Unity. Art', *Metaphysics as a Guide to Morals*, London, 1992, 8. 'The art museums, once haunted by a few experts, students and idlers, have become the temple of the Ideal, of the Other, of *something else*, that, if only for a peaceful moment, redeems our daily existence and spending. Here resides something beyond our frantic animal existence.' John Updike, *The New Yorker*, 15 November 2004, 108 (italics original).

are touched by pictures of suffering and loss. (Mass communication extends our exposure to the pain of the world. It broadens the range of our sympathy.) We weep not only at our own loss but at the loss or bereavement of others, at their grief. We are touched by tragedy. We put our hands in our pockets in time of famine when we are called upon. We not only admire nobility and generosity, we wish them for ourselves. We are revolted by hypocrisy – in ourselves or in others. We feel remorse for our meanness. We are disgusted by exploitation of the innocent, by the trafficking of humans. We are outraged when lonely old people are attacked. We want to comfort the suffering. We know tenderness. We empathise. That is our humanity.

Our Deep Self
Moral growth is about embracing and nurturing these tender movements, that is, listening to what is characteristically human about us, to what we might with some confusion call our deep self. We have been accustomed to thinking about morality as submitting our will to a wearying burden of commandments, imposed with authority and threat by society or religion. That is a trap: it gives the impression that it derives from outside us and can be cast off at will. Morality is not a fearful conformity to anyone – except perhaps to our own souls. It is that which you require of yourself, not because of some external constraints, not because of what others might think, but in order to stay true to a

particular conception of yourself and of humanity. To perform moral acts because one is afraid is not honesty: it is self-interest. One's only duty is to be human. Your soul has its touchstone. It consists of knowing that one is a thing of spirit. The truth of morality asks for something less like a submission of our will to others, and more like an opening of the imagination and of the whole mind and heart. It is a matter of going with our inner desiring.

When I mention deep self I don't mean anything esoteric. I mean this. That for much of our lives we simply go along with immediate desires and wants, led by our competitiveness, fear, envy, whatever. If we are conscious, you would have to say it is a surface consciousness or awareness, a very limited one, an automatic, reactive, conditioned response to our immediate wants and likings. It is part of our humanness to realise that to be in this kind of space is to be dominated by a very small part of ourselves. We can stand back from this. We can allow other considerations or desires to come to prominence. We can have an awareness that this is not the way to live, that this is not all of what I want in life, that there are more estimable, fulfilling desires that I could allow to come into play. There is available to me a fuller or deeper consciousness of what it means to be a person, a different level of living. Much of the moral struggle is to let this consciousness prevail and to let it become the source of more of my life. It is not a matter of high-wire intellectual activity: it is a kind

of appreciation of goodness. Some of the simplest
people have it – 'some quiet unpretentious worker, a
schoolteacher, a mother, or better still an aunt ... the aunt
may be the selfless unrewarded doer of good ... egoism
has disappeared *unobtrusively* into the care and service
of others.'[2] You can see it in this poet's tribute to an aunt:

Who, her sister dying, took on the four-year
Child, and the chance that now she would never
  make
A child of her own; who, mothering me, flowered in
The clover-soft authority of the meek ...
Of one who made no claims, but simply loved
Because that was her nature, and loving so
Asked no more than to be repaid in kind.
If she was not a saint, I do not know
What saints are ... [3]

I see it as part of our moral responsibility to *want* the
fullness of truth about living. It will be facilitated if we
find ways or strategies of listening to our deep self,
rather than busily chasing more surface desires non-
stop. It takes time and space even to *want* to listen, to
make room for the attention which invites this deeper
consciousness. Much of the spiritual practice of the great
traditions (religious, spiritual, philosophical) is about

2. Murdoch, *Metaphysics*, 429 (italics original).
3. Cecil Day Lewis, 'My Mother's Sister'.

creating a climate in our lives which will facilitate the emergence of this kind of enlightenment and desire. It is not just a matter of thinking about morality. It is about allowing our awareness to be expanded, to mull over what we have been at, to take a chance in listening to the whispers of goodness, to put faith in the wholeness of our lives, to believe that we will not be deceived or betrayed if we listen to our deepest desires.

The Autonomy of Morality

The approach which I have taken implies what you might call the autonomy of morality. By this I mean that morality makes its own demand: one should be moral because one should be moral; the call is to be human – it comes from my own true self. The question 'why be moral?' is sometimes raised. It has overtones of 'what is in it for me'? Well, it all depends on what you want from life, on what you think human living is about. The question receives as its first answer: 'because it is the human, intelligent, rational thing to do', 'because my spirit calls me to it'. It does not need any further justification. (And if someone sees no point in being rational or intelligent, in being a human being, then you are in trouble and you would probably decide that the discussion is not worth the candle.)

Some have collapsed the whole of morality into religion. They operate with the idea that it was God who gave us our moral rules. And since morality has come from God, who is creator and Lord of all things, they have a clear notion of moral obligation: God, they say, has set out the way of life which we must follow; he has ordered us to obey it; he will reward us with heaven if we do so and punish us in hell if we do not. I find that if you push people a bit about morality or its source they often, though perhaps not quite as widely nowadays, refer it back to God – probably to the ten commandments. This is rock-bottom for them.

> Mosaic imperatives bang home like rivets;
> God is a foreman with certain definite views
> Who orders life in shifts of work and leisure.[4]

Some are hooked into the view that, at some time in the past, God decided what is right and wrong, that indeed the very meaning of 'wrong' is 'prohibited by God'. Others have some sense that the right/wrong distinction is independent of God, rooted in the natures of things: God has given directives about morality, they say, but it is only to confirm and clarify matters, to confirm what our nature demands of us. Still others think of God mainly in terms of the force of morality, of obligation. They say that morality is rooted in the natures of things, and may say that we are left by God to work out the details of right and wrong, but that we are to do the right and avoid the wrong because God wills this – it is the law of God that we do so. This is what they mean when

4. Seamus Heaney, 'Docker'.

33

they use the words 'ought', or 'should', or 'cannot' in moral contexts; this is *why* we must do the right and avoid the wrong. God, for them, is the source of moral obligation.

That kind of thinking has probably faded. But still it is difficult for religious people to separate their morality from their religion. In a sense they are right: if one is a believer one's morality will be affected in various ways, as we shall see later. I will argue that we all do morality in some context: religious people do it in their religious context. But the best service we can do to morality may well be to distinguish our moral from our religious experience. There are many who are entirely convinced of the validity of the distinction of right and wrong, and who are deeply conscious of the need to abide by it, but who are religiously unmusical. But we have become so used to experiencing morality in a religious context and to having religious institutions make statements about it, that we behave as if somehow they had ownership of it, or a monopoly of it, or special insight into it. Not only do unbelievers live well but some of the most important movements for moral progress have been initiated and inspired by those who were not religious, or were even anti-religious. So we need to make distinctions between religion and morality, as we shall later.

This has become more important in recent times. The tight dependence of morality on religion has left its own doubtful legacy. Some who have more or less abandoned formal religion may find themselves struggling to locate a convincing basis for their morality. The danger is a feeling of lostness. If the religion of the fathers is abandoned – and it has often been hopelessly meshed with parental authority – does the moral code go with it? There is work to be done to clarify the ineluctable nature of morality, the responsibility that bears on every human being. If people find that morality is even more inextinguishably human than they might have thought in their religious days, that is a plus. Religion may be abandoned but the moral question remains, unless humanness is also to be abandoned. The religious believer may say that if there were no God there would be no morality, because we would not exist. But God is no more the author of the principles of morality than he or she is the author of the principles of logic. So morality does not immediately need religion: one does not need to know God in order to understand moral distinctions or obligation.

Neither does morality depend on reward. It goes without saying that many fine people who do not believe in God do believe in being moral. For them virtue is its own reward, i.e. the knowledge that they are living in the way in which they believe human beings should live. They are not slow to point out that, if they treat others justly and with respect, it is because they believe in the dignity of the other, and not because someone has told them to do so, or because they hope for some reward. They may have a point when they complain that some versions of religious morality are rather anti-morality and infantile. To collapse morality into religion, to attribute its genesis to a decree of God is to make a true appreciation of it difficult. If someone is led to believe that morality has only to do with being a Christian, or that it is something that one accepts if one wishes to ensure future happiness, then it has been devalued. It is easy to have such notions in a religious tradition. A character in one of Iris Murdoch's novels defends his atheism by claiming that religion is 'a weakener of the moral sinews'. He had a point. It can be. But it doesn't have to be.

The Authority of the Truth

The authority of morality, then, is the authority of the truth. It is independent of church, state and judiciary. It may be important, indeed indispensable, to the life of some of these institutions. Some of them may think they are good at it or know a lot about it. They may demand it from their members or subordinates. But they do not make morality and cannot make things right or wrong. They have to *find out* what is right or wrong and that can be a long and complex task: what is right or wrong, as we said, is not deduced from some abstract or eternal principle in the sky; it is discovered by reflecting on what it is actually like to be a human being among other human beings. Things are never right or wrong because somebody says so, not even God, but because of the way we are in the world, because of our human social condition. Institutions can give their opinion on moral matters. We should listen, but, as in every other area of life, the value of their opinion depends on their competence, their diligence and their honesty. So, for example, the fact that a church makes statements about war, or rights, or revolution, or the economy, or marriage, or reproduction, is important but does not in itself determine the actual morality of such actions. They are either right or wrong in themselves.

So I come back to saying that understanding characteristics or features of the human person and of society is absolutely necessary in building up ideas about what goodness means (which is why engagement with sociology and anthropology is important for morality). That means asking: what is the human importance of friendship; what is the significance of being a sexual being, what are its possibilities and pitfalls; what is it like to be without a job; what does it do to the human psyche to be discriminated against; how does it affect one's humanness to be deprived of education or culture; what does it do to a woman's sense of herself to be paid less than a man for the same job; how does it damage a child to be denied love and trust; what psychological damage is caused by child sexual abuse; what is the effect of living in a society where there is severe deprivation of a material, social or cultural kind; what is the psychic effect of years of colonialism; what is it like to be a youngster where drug pushing is rife?

Anyone can think about such matters and everyone should: from a moral point of view, what we are seeking to understand is the implications of such facts for human wholeness and flourishing, for our good, for the right conduct of all of us in society. And, for the kind of society that we need to construct, with its laws and institutions; just now in the midst of abuse scandals we find ourselves asking what kind of structures we need in both church and state if the well-being of children is to be safeguarded. Answers to all such questions are only arrived at in the gritty stuff of the everyday – by what we actually find about being human together. It is not a matter of clean lines of deduction from indisputable first principles. There should be no surprise that we disagree to some extent. Moral argument is like that. Training, upbringing and temperament enter into our assessments. We weigh goods or values or outcomes differently. Gender, too, is significant. Boys and girls have been shown to approach moral dilemmas differently. Feminist theology overturns traditional modes: it stresses intuition, community, tolerance. It has been acknowledged from the beginning of thought that moral thinking is more analogous to discussion about literature or the arts than to physics. And yet there will be considerable agreement.

So we have to share our wisdom and seek the truth for our societies. That means that adequate answers cannot be handed down by privileged people in ivory towers but only in the experience of all, and especially now, those whose voices have not been heard in the past – women, the poor, the married, homosexuals, people with disability, the marginalised. To fail to listen to them is to limit severely our moral perception and our awareness of what kind of society is needed, of where the bias and urgency of our response is to lie.

Doing What You Most Want To Do

I say again that the authority of morality is the authority of the truth, that it arises from an informed listening to our souls. I remember how struck I was when I first heard Herbert McCabe say that being moral is doing what you most want to do.[5] That goes against nearly everything we ever learned. If it sounds strange, it is because we do not know ourselves and our deep desires. If we care about being human beings we have to give time to mulling over questions like: what is in my heart of hearts; what would count as success; what is it that gives me most joy and sense of wholesomeness; when am I at peace with myself? It is a matter of wisdom, of coming to know what our real interests are. We will find that they are not just about having or winning, about something added to us externally, so to speak, like fame or wealth or popularity. That is not ultimately satisfactory. If we follow the truth, what we gain is something internal to us – fulfilment, goodness, happiness, if happiness involves for us some idea of an enriched humanness and a meaningful existence. But that requires that we allow attention to the deep desires

5. See his *Law, Love and Language*, London, 1968.

of our humanity to draw us in deeper, that we are able to distinguish between what we desire and what is worthy of our choice. Many purposes flatter and draw us. To assert that being moral is about doing what you most want to do may easily be thought of as naïve or hypocritical. It is sophisticated. It requires that we take ourselves seriously with our immortal longings.

It is, I think, useful to advert to this rich vein of goodness that is in us, since many people especially of an earlier generation were brought up to doubt it. The religious tradition in which most people of my generation were trained, and perhaps yours too, inordinately stressed self-control and discipline and appeared kill-joy. The thinking seemed to be that our desires are dangerous and wayward, that we could only with difficulty and grace keep the lid on them, and that we had to be restrained by a strict moral code heavily backed by religion and family and society. And lacing all this was the old canard that it is a struggle of soul against body, that the body and its desires are the source of our problems, and that we must ally ourselves with the mind or soul, become, as it were, disembodied. When really, as some of the Church Fathers knew very well, it is our senses that awaken us to beauty and wonder and magic – and God. It is love of the beautiful in nature and art and people, and in ourselves, that is one of our most precious gifts. It is in and through our bodies that we appreciate that we are who we are, that we express ourselves, that we say what we want to say, that we are with others. What we need is not less desire but more – greater, fuller, deeper. But our memories of fear and guilt and restraint and harshness haunt us still. No wonder we rebel against the past. No wonder we want to kick over the traces. No wonder we never want to hear another statement about morality, or a sermon about sin, or hear another priest talk about or write about sex.

> I went to the Garden of love ...
> And priests in black gowns were walking their
>   rounds,
> And binding with briars my joys and desires.[6]

So while there are sacrifices and battles in our moral lives, as we shall acknowledge, there is nonetheless a task to rescue morality, to recognise that the life of the imagination is its true home. Sadly, moral thought and concern, at least in their popular catechetical form, were cut adrift from this elemental human dynamic. When in truth it is about imagining where our heart-longings invite us to, what image of good and true and beautiful living beckons us, what a well-functioning, fair, harmonious society would be. Against the fantasy images that beguile us, we need the nourishing of a genuinely human imagination. We need to tune in to our core sense of the meaning and mystery of being a person. There is a deep opening to morality there.

6. William Blake, 'The Garden of Love'.

There are levels in moral discourse. The traditions, if not ignoring a wider virtuous living, put the emphasis mainly on the basic decencies – do not kill, or steal, or bear false witness, or commit adultery. Much of moral writing is concerned with these basic demands, as was the Decalogue or ten commandments. That is important for any society, if it is to survive. It is what will often concern me in this book. But you cannot limit moral life in this way. It cannot be caught in negatives. We all have potential and a vast world of subtle relationships. Our conduct echoes deeply in our own psyche and ripples widely in our communities and beyond: we create and support structures that enhance, or we condone structures that diminish. The call of being with others is all-embracing: we never exhaust it. Indeed, many have thought that discussing morality in terms of acts, precepts and prescriptions is very limiting. It seems to make for a minimalist response, to make morality narrowly personal, to confine it to discrete moments in life: remember the much-ridiculed 'How far can I go?'

A more open-ended approach is now preferred, one which sees moral life not as a collection of separate acts but as a *way*, as a matter of becoming a moral person. Morality is for each of us a personal journey and we don't know the journey's end. We have unique gifts and possibilities. Ideally, we might see our moral life not so much as a matter of right and wrong as of better and worse. We might have in mind, as had the ancient philosophers, the image of a perfect form of human life which beckons us forward, a virtuous life in society. That calls for a particular cast of mind and heart that enables us to judge what is best to do, and to do what is best. It is no harm to have the ideal before us, as we plod along. It is sometimes said that it is what lies behind and in between our acts that is important – that is, the readiness of our minds and hearts; that shapes what we will see, and what we will do, when the time comes. Our growth is a matter of learning to *want* some things rather than others. It is the task of educating mind and heart to love what is good.

Chapter 3
The Human Condition

S o, the business of morality is not even remotely about a set of precepts imposed on us from without. It is a matter of the human imagination, of listening to ourselves as we find ourselves. Let us grant that. But right now I want to stress something else and do so early in this book. However loftily we talk about the persistence and universality of this moral insight, we need to face fully the reality of ourselves. And, more precisely, the problem of listening to the moral call, the down and dirty stuff of life. Things are not simple. We are very complex beings. Each of us is far from being a pure and limpid fountain of moral imagination who can easily respond to our deep inspirations.

It is perhaps naïvely simple to say about us that we are a mixture and that our lives are marked by ambiguity. But I need to say something like that. We do not just have a desire to be decent and moral. We are a mass of desires. We are born with deep urges, instincts and needs. They are the very life-forces on which we depend. Take the great primordial instincts which we all have – the powerful sexual instinct, the powerful life instinct – with their attendant needs: the need for affection and esteem, the need for security and survival, the need for power and control. They are there, deeply there in all of us; we don't have to decide to have them; the only question is how they play out in our unique and different lives. They are the building blocks of our existence: without them we would not survive or relate or create or invent or love.

So we can rejoice in them and encourage them. But because they are concerned with our crucial needs, with what each of us, whether we like it or not, fiercely desires, they are troublesome, insistent. They have a deep, animal intensity. We seek in all sorts of devious ways to satisfy them. We seek power, importance, pleasure, admiration. We will do nearly anything to survive physically, or to bond and be loved, or to have some point or meaning to our lives, to count, to be esteemed, to be able to be ourselves. We may not advert to them very much: they are largely unconscious energies. They are like demons that drive us, outside our control. (Indeed some cultures have thought and still think of them as demons.) They generate great fears in us. And when we don't get, or fear we won't get, what we so elementally need, the reaction is from deep within us. We find ourselves consumed by anxiety, fear, jealousy, anger, envy, hatred and so on. We are unhinged in our emotional being. We can't help it. It is how we are made. Our emotional reaction is not a pointless, random thing. It occurs because we detect that something precious, something, as we see it, essential to us, is in danger of slipping through our grasp.[1]

The Arena of Morality: Life With Others

The point of this chapter is to acknowledge that this is what our moral life is largely about. It arises out of the very fact of our being thrown together with others in the world, and of our awareness that there is a right way, a human way, of being with them – people like ourselves, with the same basic hopes and desires and aspirations and needs, but in a world in which everyone cannot be the best, or the most loved, or the most popular, or the richest, or the most influential, or the most admired, or the most secure, or the most sure of themselves. In which everyone cannot have their needs met. In which there is competition and so conflict. So that conflict seems to be built into the very nature of our lives. After all, we have evolved from the slime of the earth. We have

---

1. 'Emotions are forms of evaluative judgment that ascribe to certain things and persons outside a person's own control great importance for the person's own flourishing. Emotions are thus acknowledgments of neediness and lack of self-sufficiency ... [they] link us to items that we regard as important for our well-being but do not fully control. The emotion records that sense of vulnerability and imperfect control.' Martha Nussbaum, *Upheavals of Thought*, Cambridge, 2001, 22, 43.

developed to plant and animal life. We carry the structure of our race's evolution – fish, bird, beast, human. We carry our biological history. We are moral beings, but withal half-beast, half-angel. A little less than the angels but sometimes a little less than the beasts too, who, it would appear, do not universally share our violence or savagery.

The irony is that it is only with and through others that we can receive the esteem and love and sense of meaning that we need. We are all unavoidably faced with a dual question. The first part is 'Does anybody love me?' and the second is 'What good am I?' The two questions belong together, because it is characteristic of us that we are not satisfied by certainty about our mere existence, and not even by certainty about our existence as thinkers and knowers. We want more; we want to be assured that we are some good – that there is some good for us or in us. It is not a matter of being 'good at'. That will not do. It is something more elemental – would you say more spiritual or metaphysical? Something about the core of being a person. We can get this assurance only by an affirmative answer to the first question, 'Does anybody love me?' And we cannot give that answer to ourselves; it comes, if it does come, from outside ourselves, from someone else. It is only if we experience ourselves as loved and valued by others that we can feel good about ourselves, feel worthy.[2] The hope always is

2. 'I receive my assurance from somewhere else ... I discover myself

that this will happen for us in the intimate relations of childhood, that the recognition we need to flourish will occur there. If sufficiently deprived of it, we cannot come to know who we are.

So we need this self-esteem and, sadly, we will do almost anything to bring it about. We may perceive that it requires from us that we show ourselves to the world as tough and unmoved. Or rich and successful. Or frail and in need of sympathy. Or pleasing and sycophantic. Or understanding and caring. Or intelligent and knowing. Or victimised and scapegoated. Whatever we imagine it takes to be noticed and valued and loved and counting. We do it deviously, of course. So there is a whole life that we hide and no doubt are ashamed of. But cannot give up. One of the desert Fathers said that the world makes us do stupid things. Well, yes. But it is not the world, it is our needs that make us do so. So what hope is there for our tender moral insight and our desire for goodness and decency? It gets lost in the toils of life.[3]

---

lovable through the other's grace; and if I finally risk loving myself, or no longer hating myself (in short, if I risk forgiving myself) I dare it through the word of the other ... through the other's mediation, and not through myself.' Jean-Luc Marion, *The Erotic Phenomenon* (Stephen E. Lewis, trans.), Chicago, 2007, 213.

3. "'It has always seemed strange to me", said Doc. "The things we admire in men – kindness and generosity, openness, honesty, understanding and feeling – are the concomitants of failure in our system. And those traits we detest – sharpness, greed, acquisitiveness,

So in exploring morality we have to take seriously the human condition, the wound of being human. If I appear to stress this, it is because I think it is unjust to neglect it. It puts unreasonable burdens of achievement on us. And it creates unfair expectations of what can be achieved through sheer will, as if anything were possible for the one of goodwill. We need to be patient and understanding with ourselves and with others – realistic, really, and we and our institutions have not always been so. Some of us have had more to endure than others. The life journey from conception to adulthood is fraught with difficulties on all sides. So much of it is out of our control and we cannot be blamed for it. We were given our genetic code. We were given our parents. We were given our early experiences. We were subjected to hurts and traumas both by those who loved us and by those who didn't. We developed our fears – that we will not survive, that we will not be loved, that we will not count, that we will die. We try to still the fear. We block out the hurt. We bury the failure. We try to ensure our security. We buy love and esteem. We wallow in our misery. We look for consolation and substitute here and there. And that gets us into all sorts of problems with others. We use them. We lose sight of them. This is how we are. This is our moral arena.

meanness, egotism and self-interest are the traits of success. And while men admire the quality of the first they love the produce of the second."'
John Steinbeck, *Cannery Row*, London, 2003, 123.

We have had different experiences, of course, in our individual and social lives. Some have been luckier than others. They have experienced warm, supportive and accepting structures – the old people, in John Montague's lovely image, like dolmens around their childhood. They have come to know love, trust, respect and friendship. Somehow they have been prepared for moral life – at least they have a good chance. Patterns of receptivity have been laid down, desires have been fostered, affections have found direction. Others have had cruel luck. They have been born into structures that crush their sense of significance and self-esteem. They have learned not to trust life, or others, or the future. They have no sense of participation, no stake in things, no sense of identity. They are inevitably and understandably anti-society: it is the only way in which they can get esteem or a sense of self-worth. They are as disabled in respect of moral possibilities as one who has lost his or her sight is disabled physically.

To reflect on such matters is not to indulge in some new-fangled New Age stuff. This kind of thinking is as old as the hills. Well, as old as the most ancient philosophers. There is nothing new under the sun. We know that one of the four great truths of Buddhism homes in on how it is desire that gives rise to suffering. But it is interesting to find an expert on the ancient philosophy of the West, Pierre Hadot – his remarks might have come from a modern meditation school – insist that it was not a dry as dust speculation, but a *practice* which was to bring about a transformation from a life of worry, fears and unregulated desires, to a more authentic way of being.[4]

So, in our confusion and bewilderment, we make inappropriate choices. We cause harm to those near us and those afar. What we do seems desirable to us at the time, it seems to be the good for us – to have fame, to be popular, to control, to get even. But it causes distress and adds to the confusion of the world. Why do we do such things? Why is it that we cannot help doing them, in spite of good intentions and resolutions? You would wonder, as generations of thinkers have wondered. Is there some propensity to evil in us, as some have claimed? A propensity to harm and destroy and murder? Or is there some evil force in the world? In his 2001 address to the Archbishop of Athens and Primate of Greece, speaking about the disastrous division of Eastern and Western Christianity, Pope John Paul II said, 'How can we fail to see here the mystery of evil

---

4. 'The philosophical act is not situated merely on the cognitive level, but on that of the self and of being. It is a progress which causes us to *be* more fully, and makes us better. It is a conversion which turns our entire life upside down, changing the life of the person who goes through it. It raises the individual from an inauthentic condition of life, darkened by unconsciousness and harassed by worry, to an authentic state of life, in which he attains self-consciousness, an exact vision of the world, inner peace, and freedom ... Philosophy thus appears, in the first place, as a therapeutic of the passions ... a profound transformation of the individual's mode of seeing and being. The object of spiritual exercise is precisely to bring about this transformation.' Pierre Hadot, *Philosophy as a Way of Life* (Michael Chase, trans.), Oxford, 1995, 83.

THE CALL TO BE HUMAN

(*mysterium iniquitatis*)'. I don't know. There are those who say that there are no truly evil people, no monsters. The philosopher Hannah Arendt caused a storm by saying that Adolf Eichmann was not a monstrously evil man but a dull and thoughtless man, and that his evil was banal: all he sought was career advancement. What you might call a surface desire. But see where it led him.

Charles Taylor puts the question forcefully: it is something that any theological account of conduct must factor in, if it is to be realistic.

> The question is this: how to understand certain powerful desires, sometimes even to the point of frenzy: wild sexuality, berserker rage, love of battle, slaughter? When we experience these, we are like wild beasts, we think. These desires are not only deeply unsettling, but also destructive. They militate against: benevolence, the binding of wounds, peace, goodness ... This wild side seems particularly strong, at least in cultures we know, among men, particularly young men. One can see their attraction to militias, fighting organisations, guerrillas, and the like. And we also note the propensity of this kind of semi-organised group violence to turn to rape, pillage, massacre. This seems to appeal as a powerful form of self-assertion, the cult of macho.[5]

5. Charles Taylor, *A Secular Age*, Cambridge, MA, 2007, 657. See Mary

Prejudices

Certainly, our needy characters lead us into harm's way. We may not have a propensity to evil but we do have a propensity to power and competitiveness, which at times serves us well, but which brings in train aggression, territoriality, possessiveness and dominance. That can lead us astray. But there are factors of a wider kind that inhibit our moral growth. Our cultural climate affects us. National, sectional and family prejudices distort our vision and our sentiments. Group prejudices, too. We know about gang culture and the inhumanities to which it can lead. We know about the killing fields. The very demeaning language of gangs and armies, and indeed of their superiors, diminishes the humanity of the other, so that killing does not mean much any more. It was part of the strategy of Nazi Germany to suggest that the Jews were not fully human: that made it easier to hate them. It was intended to dull moral perception. It was the same tactic that enabled colonisers everywhere to treat the indigenous peoples with contempt. Who knows how any of us would have behaved in such situations: the unfortunate soldier or official, who is dehumanised, becomes a victim too; solidarity in humiliating 'the enemy' becomes a way of survival.

Midgley: 'We want to understand how human conduct goes wrong. Many societies, not only ours, have considered this so grave a problem, as to call for a full-scale mythological explanation, parallel to the Fall of Man.' *Wickedness: A Philosophical Essay*, UK, 1986, 68.

This, from Doris Lessing, reflecting on her communist experience, puts it well:

> We should be careful of the company we keep and the language we use. Regimes, whole countries, have been taken over by language spreading like a virus from minds whose substance is hatred and envy. When armies are teaching soldiers to kill, the instructors are careful to put hateful epithets into their mouths: easy to kill a degenerate gook or a black monkey. When torturers teach apprentices their trade, they learn from an ugly lexicon. When revolutionary groups plan coups, their opponents are moral defectives. When they burned witches, it was to the accompaniment of a litany of calumny.[6]

I once heard a priest recount this. A woman had told him in Northern Ireland that a young British soldier had been killed in her neighbourhood. 'And you know, Father,' she said, 'I didn't feel a bit sorry for him.' Then added, 'And isn't that a terrible thing?' It is. But she recognised it: there is the struggle here between light and dark, between cultural prejudice and moral awareness. Perhaps if she had had an opportunity to come to know him and his family she would have felt differently. Frank O'Connnor's touching story, on the

6. Doris Lessing, *Under My Skin*, London, 1994, 276.

other hand, 'Guests of the Nation', tells of republican soldiers of an earlier age left to guard two British hostages destined to be shot next morning. As they whiled away the night talking and playing cards, a sense of common humanity, of fellow-feeling came over them. It was a conversion experience. So that they became unable to do the dark murder, and when they were unwilling witnesses of it next morning, the narrator remembers, his companion dropped to his knees and, as for himself, 'I was somehow very small and very lost and like a child astray in the snow and anything that happened to me afterwards I never felt the same about again'.[7] There is, I think, often a chink of light between hatred and respect, between antagonism and empathy, which can be welcomed or refused. 'There is a crack ... in everything/That's how the light gets in.'[8]

We may not have to face earth-shattering situations of war. But we all have the everyday. We can take comfort that if we get rid of our demons – the difficult and downside of our energies – we will lose our angels too: if we lose our capacity for anger or aggressiveness or jealousy or sexual bonding, we lose the thrust towards care and creativity and imagination and love; it is merely the shadow side of our moral instinct. Not to experience our demons is not to be human. It is to

7. Frank O'Connor, *Collected Stories* (Richard Ellmann, ed.) New York, 1982, 3.
8. From 'Anthem' by Leonard Cohen.

expect to be free of the energies of our lives. A carefree, pain-free, worry-free life is not on offer and perhaps our greatest mistake is to think that our 'tiny, clear/Sparkling armada of promises ... will heave to and unload/All good into our lives'.[9] But we are wrong. It is a great wisdom to accept our finite, human condition.

We have to take seriously that we are desiring beings, who are often deluded about what is good for us. Some have suggested that we distinguish surface desires – our immediate desires – and the deep desires of which the surface ones are shadows. It is a matter of organising ourselves, not of rejecting desires but of desiring more deeply and satisfactorily. So to live, that the drive for life and sex and love and meaning and creativity are organised in the way that best serves us in a community of like-minded and like-needing people. That is, in the way that our nature as a whole demands, and not in a self-defeating way that serves us ill. Or, to say it otherwise, in the way of the virtues that make for community living.

Some appear to be blessed by a natural disposition towards such virtue. But I doubt if any of us have escaped the demons that beset the human condition and that distort our being. We have somehow to diminish their hold on us. One of the great questions for the ages has been: how does one become moral? Which is the question: how does one learn to know and love what is truly our good or flourishing. How does one come to *want* that.

9. Philip Larkin, 'Next Please'.

Listen to Hadot again on ancient philosophy:

> All spiritual exercises are, fundamentally, a return to the self, in which the self is liberated from the state of alienation into which it has been plunged by worries, passions and desires. The 'self' liberated in this way is no longer merely our egoistic, passionate individuality: it is our *moral* person, open to universality and objectivity, and participating in universal nature or thought.[10]

Becoming moral is a matter of educating ourselves, freeing ourselves of delusions. But not in the simple sense of gaining information, but of being wise about being human and learning those habits of the heart which make for our peace.

Ethos

Ethos counts, as do training and environment: growth is far from being an individual affair. In fact, to try to create an ethos that is conducive to good living is about all the community can do. You cannot teach anyone to be moral. You can teach them *about* morality but you do not make them moral. Whatever moral sentiments or beliefs we have, we 'catch' from others; formal education may help to protect them from attack by others or, alternatively, enrich them, but it can never create them. As Newman put it:

10. Hadot, op. cit., 103 (italics original).

Deductions have no power of persuasion. The heart is commonly reached, not through reason but through the imagination, by means of direct impressions ... Persons influence us, voices melt us, looks subdue us, deeds inflame us ...[11]

We probably do not appreciate the significance of the whole background of our culture. I mean, in particular, the fact that different ages have scaffoldings of value within which life is lived and which subtly affect us – values of what life is about, what kind of life is worth living, what qualities are admirable, what compromises or sacrifices life requires.

They are largely unexamined, largely unconscious values. Look back at parents or grandparents and try to imagine how they saw the world, what for them went without saying, what overarching, if unthematic, scheme defined their existence. It had its shortcomings. But, compared with today – and as I write this there is anxious debate about the level of violence in our land – it had lines in the sand of shock and disgust and tolerance. Assaults on old people were unthinkable, keys were left in cars, doors were left open, the young respected their elders, teenagers did not carry knives, suicide was not in the thought of the young, the farmer helped his neighbour, you could trust your banks. The

11. John Henry Newman, *An Essay in Aid of A Grammar of Assent*, New York, 89.

climate had much to say subtly about the good life, about what is worth pursuing, about the decent thing. You would hardly call them ideals, they were too unformed for that. They were part of the air that was breathed. When such cultures fade, the effect on individual and social morality is impossible to overestimate.

Impossible Ideals
In trying to find the way between light and darkness, we need to be aware of impossible ideals: to be unrealistic here is bad for our psyche and our sense of our worth. And above all, we need to take the individual seriously. Each has suffered wounds that affect vision and heart. Each is faced with personal demons that come lurking out of the past. Ideals are useful – we *are* 'immortal diamond' – but only if they are grounded in reality and are sensitive to the personal story: individuals have their moral limitations. More broadly, there is a curious perception that Christianity somehow blames us for the fragility of our lives, for the human condition, for our native weakness. The doctrine of original sin, as it is popularly understood, has us born in guilt, already diminished, strangely responsible for our rebellious desires. What we might dwell on more positively is that, with many of the world's great foundational stories, it acknowledges the confusion inherent in us as embodied spirits, created from the dust of the earth, yet 'a little less than the angels', and by insisting that this is the fate passed on to everyone born

of woman, acknowledges the sinful social relational conditions with which we all have to contend. That could give us insight and be a comfort. But we somehow hang on to the other aspect – that we have fallen from grace, that we were not meant to be the frail creatures that we are, that we are failures. The legendary pre-Fall image of easeful self-possession – walking with God in the cool of the evening – stands in judgment on us. That, we feel, is still the gold standard for us. Unrealistic ideals are not healthy.

For all the rant about moral living, for all the sulphuric sermons of the past, it is remarkable how little thought societies and churches have given to the issue of moral conversion or growth. The energy has all gone into proclaiming and defending orthodoxy. How people might be helped to achieve the organisation of their lives, to deal with their fragility as desiring beings, has received little attention. I can only say that, if it can be done at all, it appears to me to be a much more oblique matter than teaching or preaching or threatening. Straying instinct is not easily quelled. The shimmer of excitement overcomes reason. It is difficult to be wise.

There are those who know a great deal more about moral education than I do, and I know that we need to listen to them. I can only think that it helps to sit with our patterns, to befriend our shadow, to trace back the source of our fear, anxiety and jealousy, to confront our fear of loss, to trust that there might be a greater happiness. It must help also to allow our innate goodness and sympathy to be nourished by the example of the brave and the generous around us, and by the faith and love of those gone before us. In the hope that we might catch their spirit. It is a conviction of the ancient spiritual traditions that mindfulness, meditation, attention to the reality of our own lives, leads to compassion for ourselves and others. It is deepened if we have some experience of the squalor and deprivation in which others have to live – and we don't have to go a thousand miles for that. Some sense of the unity of all things, some experience of our own vulnerability as well as that of others, leads to solidarity and commitment. It must help, too, to dwell on the great literature of the world: so much of it is a story of grief and pain, the *lacrimae rerum*, that elicits our empathy, that suggests to our moral imagination that there is enough suffering in the world without our adding to it, that moves us to feel that what is needed in the end is love.

> When I must kill a piglet, I hesitate a while.
> For about five or six seconds.
> In the name of all the beauty of the world.
> In the name of all the sadness of the world.
> 'What's keeping you?' someone bursts in then.
> Or I burst in on myself.[12]

12. Denis O'Driscoll, 'Experimental Animals'.

CHAPTER 4
Is Morality a Delusion?

I have set out the basics in chapter one. That is perhaps fine for openers. It is, I think, at least a fair starting point. But we need to look at objections. There are people who question the whole notion of morality. Of course there are people who question the particular moral code which they have inherited and been taught. The norms of Irish society and other societies have changed. If you look at recent surveys about attitudes among the young and not so young, you find that there has been a great shift in thinking about such issues as abortion, pre-marital sex, marriage, divorce etc., as well as a heightened concern about justice, about government spending, about health services, about banking, about housing, about people with disability, about mental illness, about regional imbalance, global warming, world hunger, the availability of drugs, and so on.

There have been shifts in our sense of what a genuinely moral person would look like, certainly about priorities, a rebellion of sorts against a rigid, Victorian morality – what some see as hypocrisy. The fact that people think that something is right or wrong does not make it so. But if, as they say, the *maior et sanior* (greater and saner) part of society think so, you begin to wonder if they might be right. Who else is to say anyway – authorities, philosophers, theologians? Many seem to be of the view that our authorities and professional moralists have not served us very well in the past. It is crass to say, although you sometimes hear it said, that people today are not interested in morality. You hear it said about the young. But young people today argue that they have not abandoned morality so much as rethought it in a more authentic way.

Questioning, rethinking, is healthy. Morality is the kind of discipline that requires it. The human race is on pilgrimage. But in these changing times a deeper question is raised about the very possibility or validity of morality – about what some call the objectivity of morals, although that is a term that invites confusion. The whole issue or institution of morality is called into question. Is all the talk about right and wrong just a delusion, something that we have foolishly accepted in a less questioning age, and that it is high time for us to grow out of? Is there a brave new world ahead of us in which everyone is justified in doing what they wish or feel like, in which true humanity is the humanity of freedom? Further, is something humanly acceptable if I *feel* like it, or if it feels good to me, or is what I feel I would like to do at this point?

That is a jumble of questions and it will require us to develop further our notions of morality and of its discourse. Because, about the question of the validity of morality there are different issues. You could list them somewhat like this: i) Is the whole business of morality a nonsense: should we simply stop talking about moral right and wrong and should society and educators leave people alone to do as they wish? Are moral statements fraudulent or meaningless? ii)A less radical position is that while there may be something called morality, any moral position is as justified as any other: morality is a matter of individual opinion (much like taste); so that nothing should be imposed and there can be no cross-criticism. Two related points are made. (a) Different cultures have different moralities; (b) Even within one culture we change our minds about what is right, so that morality is relative to time and place and there is nothing objective about it. Is morality not simply a matter of custom, tradition, upbringing? iii) Further to this, is it not misleading to make general moral statements because circumstances, including cultural circumstances, alter cases? They will all continue to crop up throughout this book.

The Amoralist
The first position is the most radical – that talk of morality makes no sense, that there is no validity in such talk. We call it the amoralist position. That is not just the position which says that I do not care about morality

or that I am not going to bother with it. It is the position which says that such talk is all nonsense, unjustifiable and a fraud perpetrated on us. It is the position which rejects as invalid such things as caring about other people's interests; having any inclination to tell the truth or keep promises if it does not suit one; being disposed to reject courses of action on the ground that they are unfair or dishonourable or selfish. The amoralist pays no acknowledgment to such considerations.

It is a position that is difficult enough to sustain. It usually comes with some kind of covert claim that the amoralist stance is legitimate and desirable, that it should be recognised by all. That it is alright for people to behave self-interestedly or selfishly, if they wish. At least that the amoralist does not mind if they do. There seems to be implied a *moral* notion of non-interference in the views or pursuits of others, a notion that this is how society should behave – live and let live. A morality then?

Certainly, the whole history of the human race seems to reject such a stance and has regarded it as unjustified. From the earliest times, humankind appears to have acknowledged that life cannot be lived arbitrarily, that it matters how one lives – matters to oneself and to society – and that to ignore this is to deny one's deep human inspiration or intelligence. That there is something in the very constitution of our nature that requires it. Which is why nations have been able to agree that there are kinds of conduct that are simply unacceptable, that cannot be tolerated by the world community, and for which anyone, in any culture or circumstance, can be held accountable. Even intense arguments about moral issues are indicative: they are a recognition that there is something to argue about, something important.

The diametrically opposed position to that of the amoralist is one which claims not only that there is a valid morality, but that we can have absolute and precisely stated moral rules, i.e. rules which apply to everybody, always, in all circumstances – that would say, for example, that lying, or contraception, or same-sex sexual activity is always wrong, or as it is sometimes put, intrinsically wrong – what I meant in the first chapter by getting down to the details of morality.[1] Let me call them absolute rules, or simply absolutes. In between are more nuanced positions. In order to deal with this claim of absolutes we need to pick up again the basic point from our previous chapters about our rough repertoire of needs – life, health, freedom, knowledge, self-esteem, friendship, religion and so on. They are, we said, values for us, what we consider worth pursuing. It is from our need for them, and our need that others respect them, that the broad lines of morality will emerge.

---

1. 'Intrinsically evil' is an expression that is widely used in textbooks and in church documents. It is the claim that there are some kinds of behaviour that are wrong by their very nature, in all circumstances, in all cultures, and in all times.

There is an underlying notion here of things which will bring us some – some what? I think some well-being, wholeness, flourishing, fulfilment. There is a vision of what the fulfilled life looks like. We need them for ourselves and others. We need societies of fellow human beings who will provide them – respect life, justice, freedom, truth, health and so on. And it is in our willingness to seek them for ourselves and others that our own integral fulfilment, our own genuine moral life is found. Which is not to say that there are not obscurities for any society about how they might be promoted and protected. Take, for example, questions relating to the well-being of children. Is the introduction of divorce harmful to children? Do children flourish as well in a same-sex marriage as in heterosexual? Do children need a father? Would the introduction of mandatory reporting in abuse cases be good or bad for the community; would it undermine trust? These are about facts, sociological facts, but the determination of them affects what we will see as the best choice for the community and the moral obligations of all concerned. We all find ourselves agonising about what answers to give.

We might note that statements about values are very general: nothing follows about their relative importance, about the desirability of any particular 'mix' for the achievement of a fulfilled life, about a possible clash between them – for example, is it always possible to respect both truth and life? Nor is it contended that all

67

these values are absolutely indispensable – there are cases where the pursuit of them may not be possible or desirable for an individual or society. So things are left rather open at this level of discourse. But such general moral statements are not empty: they are important for society. They form the ethos of a society. When we talk about objectivity we can take our stand on them. We cannot ignore them without denying our humanity and that of others.

All I want to do in this section is to distinguish those general, open-textured statements, from absolutes of the kind I mentioned a few paragraphs back. The point I want to make is that the objectivity of morality is not to be confused with absolute rules. It is entirely reasonable to insist that there is a moral way, a truth for living, an objectivity, in terms of these general directions or values, but to be chary about absolute rules. I take up that question more fully in chapter eleven.

The Relativist

Let us look at a less radical position than that of the amoralist. There are those who agree that morality is inescapable for human beings. But they disagree that there is any one morality. They will say that I see it one way and you see it another and never the twain shall meet. So they will maintain that there is no way of adjudicating between them, that nobody could be in a position to say that one moral position is better or worse than another. It is the position of the relativist. The most notable version of this is one which appeals to the variety of moralities in different cultures. It is an undeniable fact that cultures have come to different views about right or good living. Sexual mores differ from one culture to another: in some, polygamy is the accepted norm and it seems to work well. In some, there is strong insistence on individual human rights, in others a greater stress on social cohesion and social solidarity: so, in some, democracy is regarded as unquestioned and unquestionable, in others, more local or traditional forms of organisation work better. The relation of parents and children, the obligations of family members to one another, these differ from culture to culture. What justice means differs, or a living wage, or poverty.

What virtues are prized is in part a matter of time and culture: in earlier times excellence in battle, bravery, honour, were the prized virtues – 'come back with your shield or on it' (the Spartan mother's exhortation to her son going to battle) – in others, honesty and integrity; in others, conformity and obedience; in others, modesty and humility. Funeral orations in the time of Homer would extol different qualities from Christian burial in the Middle Ages. All this is obvious. The problem is that some argue from the *fact* of difference of moralities to the *principle* that there is no possibility of adjudicating between them or no hope of dialogue, or no justification for being critical of another culture, or indeed even of one's own, or of dialoguing with others. Or, as they say, there is no such thing as objective morality. For them, morality is a matter of whatever you are having yourself.

Another strand of modern thought poses a related problem. It can hardly have escaped the attention of anybody that we have moved out of a climate of conformity to one that celebrates individuality and difference. There was a time when people dressed mostly the same: today anything goes. There was a time when forms of behaviour were ruled by convention. Today authority of any kind – whether of custom or etiquette or protocol – is suspect. Once, in any culture, we all ate roughly the same food: now the variety becomes more bewildering by the day. There was a time when, in any one age, there were largely accepted 'styles' in architecture, art, literature, music. Change and fluidity are in possession now. Even forthright anti-styles are the fashion – the anti-novel, for example, or eclectic architectural mixtures. It is a time for the celebration of difference and diversity. The very idea of objective, universally valid experience or knowledge is rejected. Generalised concepts are especially not to be tolerated, meta-narratives, as they say: they are seen as the suffocation of individual charism and spontaneity. So, long-trusted concepts are anathema. What is troubling for all moralists is that few things have drawn the invective of these 'reformers' as fiercely as the very concepts we have been using: the notion of a common human nature and of a universal reason, which find pointers to morality in common needs and interests.

These are the key tools of moral discourse. What hope then for the objectivity of morality?

Social Construction of Reality

There is truth here but how much? There is further truth in the growing awareness of how particular ways of seeing reality influence moral judgment. We are not talking here about explicit doctrines; rather of the very social air we breathe, our largely unstructured and inarticulate understanding of our whole situation – the way our sense of ourselves is constructed, our general expectations in society. So we need to look at the social awareness out of which some of our best-known moral edicts have issued. Look at any particular age's outlook on gender, social hierarchy, power, wealth. For example, if you live in a climate which even unconsciously accepts that women are inferior to men, what conclusions are you likely to draw about their respective roles and rights? The result of centuries of discrimination is that there is an urgent need not only to promote the rights and well-being of women but to enhance women's agency in determining rights and shaping our concept of human flourishing. This will both introduce new values and relativise the values we have. Much ground remains to be made up both by community in general, by the churches, and by the theological community. In the meantime we are a stunted society. Again, if laws are made by those who enjoy power, or by those who utterly control wealth, especially if they are the influential, educated, public ones in a society, what kind of moral dispensation is likely to issue? They say, don't they, that history is written by the victors. Well, to some extent, moral mores were written by the strong and wealthy: Marx was insistent on that. Knowledge and argument can easily be tools of power. The powerful call something reality or nature when, in fact, it is merely their bias or unwarranted assumption. Just look at the morass of suffering and deprivation in which the easy assumptions of high finance have left us.

There was a time when the esteemed virtues of a woman were compliance, submission, self-sacrifice, child-bearing, and a disinclination to actively pursue personal satisfaction. It was to women that the virtues of patience, forbearance and agreeableness were especially recommended. There was a time when the plan of society was seen as divinely determined with its higher and lower orders: for both church and state it was unthinkable that it should be otherwise. It was hardly surprising then that the Catholic Church would once condemn democracy and the movement for human rights as pernicious immorality. The established order of property once dictated that any disruption of ownership was an offence of injustice: the textbooks of my youth defined restitution as the re-establishment of the old order, without question about whether the order was in fact just. Likewise, a whole culture of what was 'natural' and 'unnatural', 'normal' and 'abnormal', tolerable and taboo, infected moral judgment. Even the very inner dynamic of moral argument was skewed – a male-dominated society did not think to ask how differently men and women approach moral issues. Such prejudices have been gradually unmasked. So that a sharp suspicion of past teachings, a greater willingness to be self-critical, an awareness of our assumptions, is now seen to be crucial to the doing of morality. And also the need to modify bland assumptions of a common nature and a universal rationality. Just how much is common, just what do we assume to be rationality? As the title of one of Alasdair MacIntyre's books has it: *Whose Justice, Which Rationality?*[2] Just how much of it is, for example, the Western outlook?

All that needs to be taken as read now. But does it undermine morality? Can we not agree about anything from age to age and across cultures? Are we prepared to accept that our nature is radically and hopelessly plural? I doubt it. Human life has certain ineradicable and defining characteristics. The world-wide response to situations of distress – famine, tsunamis, earthquakes, floods, violence – suggests otherwise. As does the human community's readiness to condemn dehumanising situations. Why? What is it that we regard as unacceptable in such situations? Why do we want to change them? How come we can talk about and act cross-culturally for justice and hunger, if we have no common understanding of what a human life involves,

2. Alasdair MacIntyre, *Whose Justice, Which Rationality?*, London, 1988.

and no concepts of right and wrong? The reason we find it necessary to condemn the bias of past structures or past behaviour is precisely that we detect injustice there. It is hard to do without some acceptance that there are ways of being and acting that deserve to be appreciated and pursued by all, because they in fact lead to human flourishing. They are commensurable from one social context to another, if only analogously.

In some philosophical circles you find the proposal that the only true and valid value for us is freedom or autonomy – that the authentic human being is one who simply decides on what he or she wants to do. This, we are told, is what defines us and it is this alone that should guide our actions. This, of course, would undermine morality as we have known it. Morality becomes a matter of personal taste, of who does what and how. It is difficult to escape the conclusion that this too is being proposed as the true or authentic way. It looks very much like a truth for living. The question arises: how and why does one arrive at this one value and how come that it is the only humanly desirable one? It is an interesting fact that some who hold this radical position are often greatly interested in movements for the liberation of others (including liberation from morality). Liberation from what? And why? Why is liberation a value? Could it be that it is because it has something to do with the needs or structure of the human person. It is difficult to escape entirely notions like 'humanisation' and 'dehumanisation', 'a full humanity', 'a better state of affairs'. It is difficult to have any kind of social concern without some centering notion of human flourishing. If there is to be practical commitment to social justice and to the transforming of social institutions, or interventions in situations of human suffering – and that seems to be agreed cross-culturally – we need notions of right and wrong.

Cultures: World-View

It is possible both to respect the difference of moralities and yet hold for the objectivity of a moral order. One *does* have to recognise that to be human is to be situated in history, culture and language, and that no one can think all this away: truth comes to us embedded within sociological and cultural horizons; to be insensitive to the relativities of history is to undermine credibility. But there can be basic agreement about certain moral values and yet a varied expression of them in different times and cultures. We might say that none should live in poverty but differ on what that will mean in specific circumstances. We might agree about the importance of justice and disagree about the implications of it. The many cultures which subscribed to the UN Declaration on human rights, including the more controversial social rights, wisely refrained from pressing the point about the exact realisation of them: they envisaged a pluralism in forms of freedom, a variety of means of protecting basic rights, and different ways of resolving the tensions among rights.

So cultures can talk to one another. Rather than say that everything is utterly relative and that there can be no cross-cultural conversation, it seems more the reality that there may be agreement on basic issues but difference in their application. One might recognise that the various forms of sexual and social organisation, for example, are analogous ways of dealing with very fundamental human needs. There is no getting away from an objectivity about basic morality but much room for variation in different circumstances. As Hume put the matter: the Rhine flows north and the Rhone south but they both spring from the same mountain and are actuated in their direction by the same principle of gravity.[3] What all this means for the individual or the community is that there must be an ongoing search for the truth, a healthy suspicion of past prejudices, a provisionality about specific stances, a readiness to understand other points of view, and a willingness to see that it is through dialogue that the truth will be reached.

We might note, too, that cultures are nearer to or farther from one another in their general world-view. Between some, dialogue comes easily. But where there is a wide chasm of world-view, that is not so. It helps to advert to the fact that moral beliefs in any culture interact with beliefs of a non-moral kind. It is not easy

3. Quoted in Robin W. Lovin and Frank E. Reynolds, *Cosmogony and Ethical Order*, Chicago, 1985, 9.

to isolate moral propositions or practices from stories or myths about how things are in the world and how they came to be that way – the world-view, often religious. There are backgrounds to cultures which touch on morality: for example, one's view on human origins: on whether and to what extent we are free agents; on the source of good and evil; on what our destiny and flourishing might be; on the body; on the blessing or curse of life; on whether and in what ways we are related to one another, to non-human realities, to our past, to possible previous or future existence, to transcendence and so on. (This is not just a matter of remote cultures. There is considerable debate about the possible overlap or otherwise between contemporary religious moralities and between them and secular moralities.) Not surprisingly, Hans Küng, who has done much work in the area, stated that there can be no agreement in morality until there is agreement in religion, i.e. in world-view. That's a vain hope. But it is not impossible for religions to work together towards their own greater purification.[4]

One has to take this whole web of beliefs, the inner perspective of the culture or religion, with its own kind of consistency, in order to have an understanding of the morality which obtains. That must be appreciated. But

4. 'I can only answer the question "What am I to do?" if I can answer the prior question, "Of what story or stories do I find myself part?", MacIntyre, *After Virtue*, London, 1981, 201.

suppose it issues in practices that are understandable within the world-view of that culture but are beyond the tolerance of other cultures – one thinks of slavery, of child-sacrifice, of the killing of twins, of the belief that ageing parents should be murdered to help them to their final repose, of the danger to society of widows or witches or heretics, of female circumcision. Are such practices acceptable on the grounds that they cohere with a culture's repertoire of myths? Is one's attitude to be simply a stand-off respect – a matter of 'keeping the conversation going', as they say. Or is it legitimate to contend, without cultural imperialism, that some of these practices are simply morally wrong. Does the demand for equal respect and human rights for everyone, however difficult to agree on in its finer detail, transcend cultures? I think so. So that the need for dialogue becomes more rather than less intense. Such common search implies that there is a truth to be found, an objectivity.[5]

5. 'When we stand within the moral outlook of universal and equal respect, we don't consider its condemnation of slavery, widow-burning, human sacrifice, or female circumcision only as expressions of *our way* of being ... the moral outlook makes wider claims and this by its very nature.' Taylor, *Sources of the Self*, Cambridge, 1989, 67 (italics added).

CHAPTER 5
What Has Religion To Do With It?

So far I have been talking about morality as a demand of our humanness, as something arising spontaneously in our lives. I don't know if that is how you think of it. Some people – many until recently – have experienced it differently. They have received their morality from a religious source and see it as something dictated by a religious authority and required of them. That colours their lives in various ways. There are many excellent people who are not religious believers. They often resent the implication that their morality falls short in some way, or that they are really crypto-believers who need God for their sense of moral obligation. And, increasingly, there are those who regard religious morality – what they see as a belief that God has issued a set of rules and imposed moral obligation with fearful sanctions – as infantile, as an anti-morality which reduces believers to the condition of fearful children, and reduces morality to a craven subjection to

God's will. Religion is even more seriously pilloried as a malevolent influence, as the enemy of morality, the cause of crimes, wars and slaughter. So there is understandable reference to the Crusades, the religious wars, the Inquisition etc.

Whatever about such fateful issues, the effect of religion on the more personal aspects of the lives of believers is also a concern. My interest here is mainly the morality of Christians, but it is well to recognise that such morality is only one instance of a wider phenomenon, i.e. religious morality – Muslim, Jewish, Buddhist and so on. The question for us – and it will overhang succeeding chapters – is this: if one is a religious believer, what effect will that have on one's morality? And beyond that, is religion an intruder in the moral area; can one justify its role; is it likely to enhance moral life or the opposite; will it render agreement on moral matters impossible for people of different religious persuasion or of none? Should church leaders, as they are often advised, confine themselves to their sacristies?

Religion and Morality
Not that religion and morality are alien. They are cousins. Indeed many see morality as raising the religious question: they have a sense that its rootedness in our humanity, its concern for goodness and beauty of life, for rationality and order, its demanding nature hint at the question whether it has some ultimate source,

or meaning, or context, of a religious kind. But it is useful to distinguish the two. The general notion of religion is vague enough. But, in general, its significance is that it is a system of beliefs and practices by means of which we struggle with the ultimate problems of existence: why are we here; where do we come from; for what purpose; why do we act in this way; why do we die; what is our destiny; what is our salvation? Many see it as illuminating the longings and aspirations, the fears and loneliness of the human heart; they find that it speaks to their restlessness and their thrust towards truth and love. In the Christian tradition that crystallizes around belief in a personal God, who is source of life, last end, the fulfilment of desire, and someone who has certain attributes such as perfection, goodness, rationality etc.: 'O Beauty ever ancient, ever new';[1] 'Our heart is restless until it rests in you'.[2]

What is fundamental to a religion is its faith/story/ myth, which addresses such questions. The basic myth – and its satellite myths – if sincerely assented to, affects the life of the individual in deep and different ways. It touches on issues of meaning – is there any point or destiny to life or is it just one thing after another? It colours attitudes to others, to bodily existence, to death – is love, pleasure, flesh, sex, good or bad? It shades one's emotional condition – joy or despair in life, trust or fear,

---

1. Saint Augustine, *Confessions* (Henry Chadwick, trans.), Oxford, 1991, 201.
2. Ibid., 3.

hope or emptiness. Do we think that God's in his heaven and all's right with the world or do we live in fear? It throws light on the trajectory of human existence – is it in the end nothingness or fulfilment? It determines the relative importance and significance of action, of success or failure – it was very much the Irish tradition to caution children to keep their faith above everything else. So it bears on what might be called our deepest anxieties in a marked way. If it does, it is likely to have an effect on morality. I am not saying that non-believers do not have meaning and a range of emotion; only that a religious faith gives its own colour to them.

Because there has been a tendency to narrow religion to morality, it is important to dwell on these more profound implications of the religious stance – religious faith and morality are related but they are not to be confused. I find that many regard the matter of having a morality or a special and typical morality as the whole point of religion. If one suggests that the morality expected of Christians is the same as that expected of the good humanist, the anxious question often arises: what then is the point of being a Christian? Well, there is a point. The point is the deeper matter of one's existence, of meaning, of human aspiration. It is a pity that religion has tended to be narrowed to a moral code. That empties it of much that is valuable. That may be why some have abandoned formal religion in favour of what they call spirituality – because it does not offer them the spiritual sustenance they need. And why others have done so because they see it as responsible for a discredited morality.

What we find is that we have to deal with two great strands of human experience, the religious and the moral. They both command our allegiance: we commit ourselves to our religious world-view, and we also believe that we should obey our moral sense or conscience. Religious faith or charism tends to become organised in an institution. The religions of the world find expression not only conceptually but emotionally and practically. So they propose or insist on the acceptance of a myth (what we believe), the practice of a cult (the prayers, worship, rituals we have), an organisational system (we might have an authority, priests, prophets, privileged people) and the observance of a set of action guides (the moral behaviour that is expected). That is to put the matter very generally: one could argue for other common characteristics. What matters for our purposes is to note that religions attach a different weight or significance to these elements: even within any one religion the significance varies from one period of its history to another. And also, if our religion proposes a moral system, we must wonder about how we are to understand this – since we have insisted that morality is an experience that arises autonomously for human beings. What are the implications of such 'religious morality'? Certainly, a strong moral sense is something that is greatly admired: fidelity to moral truth in the face of threats, punishments or enticements has generated heroic witness in every age. What then if a religion appears to colonise this area? What if there appears to be a clash, if the dictates of our religion and our morality are in tension – is it to be religious obedience or moral insight?

The different elements in a religion do not stand distinct from one another. They are held in an overall attitude to life, a kind of ethico-religious ethos, something both imaginative and moral which shapes the believer's outlook. Within that, much needs to be teased out.

Because religions differ in their central stories or myths, they will differ in how they understand and deal with morality. Much depends on their notion of the deity. In some religions, the deity is personal, good and benign; in others, the deity is in some respects evil. In some, the deity is otiose or indifferent and creation is devoid of moral purpose; in others, the deity is the guide of human history. If your deity is capricious or morally indifferent, your religion might not give high priority to morality. For Christians, however, the story is one of a deity who is an intelligent and purposeful creator and sustainer, a moral being who has a care for his/her people, a purpose in history, a covenant with the whole of creation. There is therefore in Christian religious stories an inner impetus towards morality, towards engagement with others and with the structures in which they live.

This appears strikingly in what for both Jews and Christians remains a foundation document – the giving of the law to Moses. What is central in that account is that the people of God were to be a moral people. Their God was a good God. They too were to live moral lives. Their religion would be moral and their morality religious. Living morally or failing to do so, listening to their native moral call or rejecting it, involved them with God. It had an ultimate significance beyond itself. That is the insight of the Moses story – that, rather than the actual moral content. It was a message that the prophets hammered home.

> Will the Lord be pleased with thousands of rams,
> With ten thousands of rivers of oil ...?
> What does the Lord require of you
> But to do justice, and to love kindness,
> And to walk humbly before your God.
>
> (Micah 6:7-8)

> Even though you make many prayers,
> I will not listen ...
> Cease to do evil, learn to do good;
> Seek justice, correct oppression;
> Defend the fatherless, plead for the widow.
>
> (Isa 1:11ff.)

When we come to the New Testament we find the same tension of ritual and behaviour. If you come to offer your gift at the altar but are at odds with your brother or sister, go and be reconciled and then come to offer your gift. If you ask what is the greatest commandment, the answer is that it is to love God and your neighbour. If you ask who will possess the kingdom, it will not be those who put their faith in ritual practices or trust in descent from Abraham, but those who give to the hungry and thirsty, who visit the sick and imprisoned. Christian living is inescapably moral. Christian spirituality must engage with the everyday: we are to love as God loved us in Christ. That gives the general *élan* of Christian life. That is its spirit: anything else is escapist. It is a fair question to ask how this meshing of religion and morality was played out in succeeding ages.

Religion Affects Morality

When you ask how religion affects morality you find yourself with several questions. Let us then do a bit of dissecting. We might inquire whether a particular religious faith affects, perhaps even diminishes, the *very notion of morality and moral obligation*. Or ask about its views on the possibility of *knowing* the demands of morality, whether, for example, it believes that it needed and has received a special *revelation* about moral living. Or about how it *interprets* the whole moral enterprise or *supports* it, or offers *motivation* for it, or provides an impulse to it. Or about the *significance* of moral life within the faith, since the moral strand receives a different emphasis from one religion to another. What is of greatest interest to most people, I think, is what the religion has to say about the *kind of conduct* that it considers appropriate or necessary – whether it has a basic behaviour code, a disciplinary requirement for belonging, and whether it regards its moral code as in some way specific. Do Christians require or expect or praise a conduct that is different from what Hindus or Muslims or humanists require or expect or praise? I'll consider that in the following chapters. But there is perhaps a more important question, that of the bearing of religion – and let us look at Christianity now – on the *notion* of morality and moral obligation.

What Christians have imbibed down the ages, at least until very recently, is that morality comes from God, that he/she is its source and its force. Worse, that he/she is a lawgiver and a punisher of the morally wayward. It is here more than anywhere else that a question arises about the influence of religion – benign or malevolent? It merges into another of the questions, that of the *place* of morality in Christianity. It has to be admitted that there was and is a problem. It is this. While Christians can maintain a relative autonomy for morality they cannot regard it – any more than anything else in life – as absolutely autonomous. They cannot say what they want to say about the world and all its immanent activity and institutions without referring it to God. They cannot see morality solely as morality. They must somehow express their belief that it is God's world, that the institution of morality is consonant with God and his purposes, that, so to speak, it is part of what God willed human beings to discover about themselves. This is something that is difficult to express. We are engaged with a species of God-talk: we'll see further examples of it in the next chapter. All God-talk is the use of our human language to suggest something that is not entirely within the range of our experience: we can know what we experience but we cannot fully know who or what God is. So we are stuck with applying terms from our daily life to God. At best they will be inadequate, at worst seriously misleading.

The Law of God

The manner of expressing this which became most common for Jews and Christians was to say that the moral code was an element of the treaty between God and his people. It was the *law* of God. This way of expressing it was accentuated in a medieval world that was very conscious of the relations of lord and servant, a lord who gives orders, organises the life of his underlings, and punishes those who do not conform. The textbooks and catechisms that have dominated Christian history were locked into this culture of law. They went to some trouble to prove that morality qualifies for the strict notion of law, with its paraphernalia of lawgiver, promulgation and sanction. They were doing the best they could to make sense of the complexity of religion and morality. But they were giving hostages to fortune.

The insistence on morality as law, while under-standable, is fraught with problems. There is a danger of thinking of morality as a code of conduct coming from outside us, made by someone in authority and enjoined on us. That is how we usually think of a law: it runs counter to what we have been saying up to now. God does not make morality, nor is it from God that the obligation of morality comes. Morality is a matter of the human spirit: that is where its demand comes from. Honesty, for example, is good in itself: it makes its own demand; but it can be – and, for Christians, may need to be – called the law or will of God. Cruelty is wrong in itself but it can be said to be contrary to the will of God. God makes us, but it is we who discover the moral dimension within ourselves. So whatever 'law of God' language might mean, it does not mean that morality or its binding force derive from God. In fact, it is much more native to and constitutive of us than any external command or law, even from God. In that regard Christians can be at one with and can dialogue with humanist moralists.

There are more nuanced understandings of law. For the great scholastics it signified inner guidance towards an end, towards one's good. I could, in this sense, refer to morality as the law of my being, as my inbuilt awareness of the sacredness of others, as the thrust in me towards my good or flourishing. And I could say that, in this sense, morality is the law or will of God my Creator. But there is all the difference in the world between thinking of human beings listening to a thrust in themselves to behave in a particular way and finding it appropriate to refer to this also as the will or law of God, and thinking of morality as the law of God because

THE CALL TO BE HUMAN

it is a set of ordinances issued by him/her. 'Law of God', then, is a kind of short-hand or metaphor which we use to describe a complex cluster of ideas.

It is always a problem for religions when the original charism or inspiration becomes institutionalised in a wider church. Who's in, who's out, who's right, who's wrong, who's ours, who's theirs – who is in heresy and who is not – all becomes an issue and discipline assumes importance. That is what happened in Christianity. The moral element, with its law metaphor, took over, ever expanding, ever more insistent – now the touchstone of membership. However it happened, the image that was handed down was of a God prying into every nook and cranny of life, and of a church flushing sin from the coverts of our souls. How did we get from the Spring flower of the New Testament to the sick worry of the confessional?

> Being sent to penance, come Saturday,
> I shuffled slower than my sins should,
> My fears were candle-spiked at side-shrines ...
> Did I
> Take pleasure, when alone – how much –
> In a bad thought, immodest look,
> Or worse, unnecessary touch?
> Closeted in the confessional
> I put on flesh, so many years
> Were added to my own ...[3]

3. Austin Clarke, 'Ancient Lights'.

There are many sad stories. It would be hard to measure the anxiety that bore upon people. Or the deadening weight of submission that it imposed. No wonder there is anger. Too long a suffering makes a stone of the heart.

I sometimes hear radio discussions on Christian morality and what is pilloried is nothing that I recognise as Christian morality today: it is a caricature. That is annoying. But, at the same time, one cannot but agree about the baleful effects of the past – the enervating fear before an all-threatening God. It is true that fear may have prevented harm in the community – if we could stop people killing or maiming one another, fear might be a small price to pay – and there are those who regret its passing. And it is true that today many appear rudderless without the influence of religion. But the confessional discipline obscured the true meaning of morality. It did little for moral growth. It even trivialised moral failure. It engendered unwarranted guilt. The troubling question is why it went unchallenged for so long. Why the kindlier Christian tradition which saw moral failure more as weakness than as crime, and saw God – and indeed the confessor – more as healer than as judge, was buried almost without trace. That is a reproach on us all. It says much about the inherent danger of institutions that brook no questioning.

The language of 'commandment' remains ambivalent. It is nearer the truth to see the Decalogue story as urging us to listen to our native moral call, and thus be part of the unselfish love of God for all humanity. When we fail, it is others that we fail: it is our obligation to the world and its humanisation that comes up short. That must be the first target of our sorrow. It is first to one another that we are to recognise moral failure, lament it, and, if possible, remedy it. But the Christian is aware that, in the broader context of our lives, that is a rupture in our relation with God: it is to fail the plan of God, God's covenant with creation, the mission of Christ, the promptings of the Spirit – whatever about our difficulties in finding a satisfactory language to express this God–morality relationship. It is this context that makes sense of the language of sin – the other side of law. Sin is not something created by God or the church. It is absence of love, failure of soul, refusal of human wholeness. But for Christians it has a God-dimension.

It is sad that it was in the Christian sacrament of reconciliation that the religion-morality dilemma had its most harmful effects: for the older generation it was often a deeply distressing experience. It did not have to be so. It is meant to offer us a sacred place to deal with our depressing experience of failure. It is a gesture towards our bodiliness, our need for ritual. It is an invitation together to share the frailty of the human condition, to pray together for healing and harmony, to remember together that our faith's deepest-down conviction is that the ground of our being is under-standing of our vulnerability. We have the hope that death will not see the end of life but will bring the promise of a closer relationship to our Creator. That only, nothing of fire and judgment. Where or when or how we do not know. Nor is there any knowing of how the loving-kindness of God, which both Testaments celebrate, encompasses even our failures.

> Nay, Lord, not thus! white lilies in the spring,
> Sad olive groves, or silver-breasted dove,
> Teach me more clearly of Thy life and love
> Than terrors of red flame or thundering.[4]

Many other questions remain for the following chapters about religious, and specifically, Christian, morality. But let us sum up this one. It is possible to speak of morality, of duty, of moral claim, of conscience, without referring to God – and many do. But it is not possible for a believer to express adequately his/her total view of things without making some attempt to contextualise all things, morality included, in God. To refer to morality, then, as the law or will of God, or imitation of God, or reign of God, or in some such religious terms, is for the Christian a necessary description of the world. But the language of 'law' or 'will', with which we are familiar in our daily lives, cannot be transferred without great logical caution to God and morality – it has been described as 'a baffling semantic task'.[5] The will of God is not written in the skies or in some decree he/she has

---

4. Oscar Wilde, 'Sonnet on Hearing the *Dies Irae* Sung in the Sistine Chapel'.
5. Bernard Williams, *Morality: An Introduction to Ethics*, London, 1972, 85.

given in the past, or in some direction he/she gives now. No, whatever is morally right is the will or law of God, whatever is wrong is contrary to the will of God: 'all that is true, all that is noble, all that is just and pure, all that is lovable and gracious, whatever is excellent and admirable – fill all your thoughts with these things' (Phil 4:8). If we have discovered the morally right we have *then* discovered the will of God. We do not do justice to the notion of morality unless we somehow preclude the deduction that God is a man with a 'will', who issues commands like a ruler or sergeant-major, who invigilates our every moment, and who arranges for punishment for those who do not obey.

CHAPTER 6
Should We Take the Bible Seriously?

A re we to listen to our religion about what is right and wrong? Certainly, religions take it on themselves to direct their adherents: the acceptance of their moral code is often regarded as a necessary condition of membership. Religions also seek to influence public debate. We have had several examples of the engagement of the churches in debates about war, the economy, abortion, medical experimentation, stem-cell research and so on. Non-religious constantly decry this as interference. They see it as a struggle between genuine morality and religious dogmatism. We ask then: how does religion bear on behaviour, on the *content* of moral behaviour: why are churches so interested in morality, private and public; and why do they feel some special competence in moral matters? Especially since we have argued for the autonomy of morality.

We have seen that, for the believer, morality cannot remain just morality. It has to be in some way related to God. What then have Christians made of it? Churches do not think up their community life from scratch, from age to age. We live in a tradition and the bible is the classic of the tradition, its foundation, and for all Christians it is the word of God, and in some sense authoritative. It has a strong ethical spine but its ethical material is diverse. The question for us is: is it God's revelation of the moral way, or in what sense is it authoritative in moral matters? The bible is a confusing diversity. Its mode is indicative, imperative, parabolic, mystical. It is more story than history, more gospel than law. It says what it has to say in a bewildering profusion of forms and genres, so that it is hard to know what to make of it. But Christians have confidence, nonetheless, that in the biblical sayings and stories of the early church, we have testimonies to traditions which were shaped by the impact of the historical Jesus. Not to engage with this is not to know our lineage, not to know who we are and how we are to be.

You could tease out what we may roughly call the ethical material. Some of it seems to give us clear directives about living. Take, for example, the saying attributed to Jesus that he who leaves his wife and marries another commits adultery: for some churches that is compelling teaching. Some of it is more obliquely related to morality. It is rather talk about God. It tells us about the *source* of moral goodness – the love of God is poured into our hearts, the Spirit is given to us – or about its ultimate *significance*   'Come you blessed of my Father ... as long as you did it to one of these you did it to me.' It offers us powerful *motivation* for right living: God's action in Christ is to be an inspiration for our lives. It has symbols and stories that *support* the moral endeavour, notably stories of hope, of the Suffering Servant justified, of death-resurrection.

> Although the fig-tree does not burgeon,
> The vines bear no fruit,
> the olive crop fails
> the orchards yield no fruit,
> the fold is bereft of its flock
> and there are no cattle in the stalls,
> yet will I exult in the Lord.   (Habakkuk 3:17)

A great deal of this material is more religious context than moral information. But it has a bearing. If I make distinctions between these elements, I don't want to push it too far. The different aspects shade into one another and we are to live our lives in their general climate. But the distinctions can be useful.

Faith Bears on Morality
It is the *directives* of the bible, the occasions when it seems to tell us precisely what to do, that most engage the churches and are most controversial. I will give them separate treatment in the next chapter. But I think it is

97

a mistake to concentrate on them. However significant they may be, they are not the whole story. More important is the subtle but indirect way in which the bible, like any cultural tradition, bears on our lives. That, I think, is what should particularly interest us as Christians. I am talking about its spirit or ethos. I suppose you would call it biblical faith rather than biblical morality. Its great stories have suggestive things to say to us about what it means to be a human being, about the value of the human person, about the meaning and significance of history, about life and death, about what constitutes flourishing or perfection, about blessedness, about success and failure, about sin and sinfulness. It tells us who we are. It doesn't spell it out in theories or statements. That doesn't matter: after all, our songs and stories are more powerful in creating a sense of who we are than our constitution or laws. So, too, with faith stories and faith consciousness. What they do is create an imagination. That bears on our moral sense, for moral judgments are not made in a vacuum. They are made by people who see life in a particular way. To belong to a religious community is never incidental to one's self-understanding or perception of reality. It gives us our outlook about the way things are and about what is important: and thus it shapes our identity and influences our decisions.

You can see in the early Christian community how faith had this formative effect, how it had the potential to form a particular kind of community. Its character was shaped by the memory of what God had done for it in Christ. There is a dynamic relationship between the liturgical recital of the great story and moral expect-ations. 'If then our common life in Christ yields anything to stir the heart ... fill up my cup of happiness by thinking and feeling alike, with the same love for one another, the same turn of mind and a common care for unity ...' (Phil 2:1). 'All whose faith had drawn them together held everything in common: they would sell their property and possessions and make a general distribution as the need of each required. With one mind they kept up their daily attendance at the temple ... (Acts 2:44ff.). Perhaps that does not give anything like clear directives for living, but it creates a climate and imagination.

We share the faith of those first Christians. We are faced with problems analogous to theirs in the raw towns in which we live and die. Different times, different places, it is true. So there will be no facile answers. But we can allow that same faith-view to enrich our ethical imagination today. Their basic stories enclose our lives. It is illuminating for us then to enter into a back and forward dialogue with them, with their account of what the inbreak of the reign of God in Christ meant for their daily life, as we seek to discover the logic of faith for our own day. We need to let the bible bear on us, to live in that atmosphere, to breathe the same air. It is this looser, more indirect bearing of the bible on our lives that for me is the primary point of reading the bible, of joining study groups, of praying.[1]

The Biblical Spirit

If we do enter into the God-story we will be struck by the fact that the early community was concerned about wayward desires, about filling our barns, seeking the first places, winning men's favour, wanting to lord it over others – about the dark forest of the heart. It had paradoxical things to say about the need to die to self, about losing and finding one's life, about one's true self. It overturned accepted patterns of striving, seeking and possessing. It recommended a style of poverty of life and spirit, of seeking the interests of others and not one's own, of giving to everyone who asks, of turning the other cheek, of peacefulness, of washing one another's feet, of trust in God, of being prepared to lay down one's life for others. It had a special place for the poor and the marginalised and despised. It is the source of a fundamental humility, which saves us from over-valuing our own gifts, over-esteeming our own opinions

1. 'We find what is perhaps the very kernel of the phenomenon of civilisation – a collection of images and symbols by which a human group expresses its adaptations to reality, to other groups and to history ... One could speak in this sense of the ethico-mythical kernel, the kernel both moral and imaginative which embodies the ultimate creaturely power of a group.' Paul Ricoeur, 'The Tasks of the Political Educator', *Philosophy Today*,17 (1973),146.

and placing excessive importance on getting our own way. It shows us our place in the cosmos: it decentres us. We are not the fulcrum of the world and it does not exist to be exploited by us. You could call them evangelical values.

All of this is morally significant. Much of it is carried by what some call the indicative-imperative of the gospels, that is, by the way in which what God does suggests what is appropriate for us. God welcomes the stranger, liberates the oppressed, forgives and blesses enemies, makes his/her sun shine on the unjust and just alike. ('You shall not deprive aliens and orphans of justice nor take a widow's cloak in pledge. Remember that you were slaves in Egypt and the Lord your God redeemed you from there.' Deut 24:17) We are to learn from that. Christ emptied himself to come among us: we are to be servants of others. We have received the Spirit: we should bring forth the fruits of the Spirit. There is so much of this kind of dynamic. It both inculcates a wisdom for living and inspires to moral effort. The scripture scholar Joachim Jeremias puts it strikingly. The mistake we make about the high demands of the Sermon on the Mount, he says, is that we leave out the story – the story that we ourselves have first been forgiven in Christ. Because 'your sins are forgiven' (so Jeremias puts it) there now follows, 'While you are still in the way with your opponent be reconciled to him quickly'. 'Because your sins are forgiven' there now follows 'Love your enemies and pray for those who persecute you'. We are seduced into forgiveness. The Beatitudes hold out tantalising promises that this is the direction in which blessedness and wholeness are to be found. The best of psychology, I think, would agree.[2]

If I say that some of these orientations tend to be vocational matters, I mean only that good living admits of different emphases: for some they will be the decisive feature of life, as for those who vow themselves to a life of poverty. But Christians generally are called to turn the other cheek, go the second mile, give to everyone who asks, forgive as Christ forgave. These are dramatic gospel examples, to be taken seriously if not literally. How precisely they are to be interpreted differs from age to age, from person to person, from possibility to possibility. But they are not just for an elite. We all need them and, as the daily carnage of war and revenge mounts, as economic lunacy deepens, as political exploitation spreads, the world needs those who take them seriously. Pope Benedict XVI, in his latest encyclical, hopes for an economics characterised by relationships of gratuitousness, mercy and communion. It may not cut much ice with big business but for Christians it is a call that has the ring of the gospel about it.

This is the distinctive Christian way. I don't mean specific or altogether different from others at this point,

2. Joachim Jeremias, *The Sermon on the Mount* (Perrin, trans.), London, 1961, 36–47.

and I don't mean better. We have seen in earlier chapters
that an analogous style of living is part of a universal
wisdom. What I stress here is that it coheres with the
Christian story and what matters is that Christians be
faithful to their own ethos. It creates a way of understanding one's being in the world. And, while it may not
give precise direction, it is at least an ever-present
reminder that there are acts, intentions, dispositions and
purposes that run entirely contrary to Christian
sensibility. For example, it makes no sense to subscribe
to the Christian story and fail to realise that life is a good
gift, that each human being is precious, that we are to
be community-builders, that the poor, the weak and the
outcast are to be especially protected, that we are to be
respectful stewards of creation. That is the logic of faith.
You could not really claim to be a Christian if you were
not in some way affected by this. It calls you forward.
You may not do anything about it, but it will hang like
a judgment on you.

Clearly, it is a morality of ideals. A morality not just
of acts but of the heart, or of inner disposition – for the
undeveloped heart is a matter of moral reproach. He
who lusts after a woman has already committed adultery
with her in his heart: it is not the outside of cup or dish
that matters. A morality of virtue then. Not just about
the demarcation of right and wrong, however important
that might be at times. But about better and worse. And
yet a morality of realism. In its own way, it has much to
say about our temptation to self-aggrandisement of a

political or sexual or intellectual kind, about respecting riches, not wanting to know our poor relations, being enclosed in one's own ambitions, harbouring resentment. It takes sin seriously, the stubbornness of sin – those frailties of our personal and social lives that make it hard for us to see and love the true way. It recognises the build-up of prejudice and irrationality over the ages, the sin of the world – the cruel, unjust and selfish structures that breed resentment and violence and cloud the vision of all of us.

It is not that one can easily lift out of the bible clear solutions to today's problems. The much cited 'doing what Jesus would have done' will not yield easy and immediate answers. We cannot easily shell out the essence of Christian life from the culture of its time and pop it into our own times. There will be useful analogies to be found, there are clues, suggestions, orientations, but they must be treated with care. Obviously, there are problems today to which the bible does not offer any solution. And yet in this kind of conversation the main lineaments of the Christian way can be discerned and can influence us. We have enough of a hold of the early community's vision of Christ to have guidance on our way. It is not all sunshine. There is throughout a call for conversion. I take that to mean a re-education of desires, an awareness of our own blindness, and what I have referred to in earlier chapters as a deeper consciousness or enlightenment. Provided we don't think that enlightenment is a matter just of knowledge. It is something that carries truth alive into the chambers of the heart, something that dissolves bitterness and selfishness and the fog that enwraps us. Something that enables change, that makes us want to be good.

This is not some wishy-washy stuff. It will be said to be vague – and that does not suit an authoritarian or legal mentality – but the imagination of it is much more powerful than the heavily weighted pronouncements that have marked our ecclesiastical history. It is interesting to ponder on it today when there is a sudden awakening to our need radically to reform our politics, economics, medicine and law. Every second commentator, every second letter to the papers, is preaching it, with a zeal that would flatter an Old Testament prophet. The call is for values. For virtues, really – for trust, honesty, community, respect for the individual, restraint in the pursuit of wealth, appreciation of the genuine things in life. For a check on competitiveness, on easy gain, on exploitation. Well, you find it all in the bible. Again, I am not saying that others do not or cannot have these perspectives and values. Obviously, they do. Only that Christians must have them if they are to be true to their faith and liturgical life.

Do I have to say that the message can be easily distorted? Throughout history, the Christian churches in some respects took on the paraphernalia of the societies they found themselves in – curias and chancelleries and palaces and so on – and moved a long way from the spirit of the carpenter of Nazareth. It is a bad thing to forget your origins. But the message became more seriously distorted in other ways. Of course, you can never get the ice-pure gospel. It is embedded in the cultures from which it sprang. Their thought-patterns and prejudices show through. Over time, ersatz religious movements, political consider-ations, and the allure of power, further dulled the early brightness. So that, for example, war became acceptable and gave rise to endless manipulation. So that structures, discipline and order ruled over spirit. So that the glad morning was overcast by the clouds of heresies, some with their weird slant on life and body and sexuality. 'A sense of the presence of "Satan", in the form of a constant and ill-defined risk of lust lay like a heavy shadow in the corner of every Christian Church.'[3] Which led, over time, to a disparagement of senses and feelings, a suspicion of passion, and an exaltation of detachment – to the detriment of more important virtues. The result was a skewed notion of morality and spirituality, which has done great harm even in our own time. We must ever be reaching back in hope to find the true spirit of the bible and seek to reform ourselves in the light of it. The church must ever be renewing itself.

A Stance

What does this acceptance of the bible mean then? Does it mean that we meekly take what the bible tells us? That

3. Peter Brown, *The Body in Society*, New York, 1988, 55.

we fall under the censure of those who reject religious morality as a childish fear of the deity, as unthinking subservience, as destructive of autonomy and intelligence? No. The great spine of moral response, rooted in the human spirit, remains secure with us. Our down-here human search continues. But it is people of a particular vision who search. We don't confront life as atheists or agnostics. We allow the outlook and spirit of the bible to colour our world-view. That impinges on our search. Some critics of religion would like to claim that they are the only ones who take a pure, unprejudiced, rational approach to morality, and that anything else is suspect. There is no such thing as such an approach. There is no escaping a *prise de position* on the great shaping questions of life. The agnostic or atheist or nihilist position is a *position*: it is no more rational than any other. It too has a stance about the world, the person, the meaning of life, the possibility of hope, the significance of death. It works out of its own unproven presuppositions. Many, of course, disagree with the Christian world-view. There is no quarrel about that. One can only hope for tolerance, for freedom of thought, for dialogue in the service of the truth. There are encouraging signs of that today in the search for a world ethic.

As Christians we do not engage uncritically, we do not abandon our intelligence and awareness of change and culture. We have to work with what has been handed down. It will not be a matter simply of applying some biblical perspectives to today's issues. Indeed, the reverse is often the case: it is in and through the experiences of today that the meaning of the bible is revealed to us; this was a key insight of liberation theology and it has analogies in feminist and black theology. It is only in the sorrow and suffering of life, in the hurt and the forgiveness, as well as in its joy and ecstasy that we discover what biblical liberation and justice and hope and love and salvation mean. I think it was Metz who said that we cannot do our theology with our back to Auschwitz. Nor can we do it with our back to more recent outrages, such as the scandal of child-abuse. All human life is waiting to be illumined by the bible. Vague aspirations of love or concern will not see us through either. We have to find out what love means, or humanisation: we have to have a suspicion of our own assumptions; we have to see where the greatest needs are; we have to search for the causes of sin and oppression; we have to devise political strategies; we have to seek light on the problems of evil, failure and death; but in doing so it would be a mistake not to remember who we are, not to see ourselves in the lineage of the Christian story carried down to us from those who had experience of the Lord.

CHAPTER 7
'But It Says in the Bible ...'

What is interesting is what Christian churches have made of the diverse material of the bible. They have, of course, proclaimed the vision. They have encouraged the great virtues which go with it. They have exhorted their members to generosity of life. All of that is to the good. But churches have not settled for this open and imaginative approach to the bible. They have nailed things down much more firmly. They look to the bible for exceptionless binding directives. 'It says in the bible' has led to rigidity for individuals and institutions. We see it very vividly today in the debate on marriage and homosexuality in the Anglican communion, with one side wanting 'to reassert the authority of the bible'. It has long been associated with other Protestant churches – take, for example, the observance of the Lord's Day – and has been a crucial and controversial element of Roman Catholic official teaching.

There will not be much debate about the general, open-textured exhortations of the bible – 'be merciful', 'give to everyone who asks', 'always be grateful', 'do not swear', 'do not lay up treasure on earth', 'do not worry about tomorrow'. For one thing, such exhortations, while they are part of the Christian spirit, admit of different realisations from age to age. For another, they are widely regarded, even by Christians, as in some respects matters of supererogation or heroism. The main Christian churches do not impose them. No one is likely to object if another decides to live a life of poverty or simplicity or trust in God. Someone who does not share the Christian world-view may regard it as foolish, but that is probably as far as it will go. It is also worth noting that it is part of the wisdom of many of the great spiritual traditions, particularly of the East, to extol a life of simplicity, detachment, compassion and peacefulness.

A Revealed Morality of Rules

Permanent and exceptionless rules are another matter – I mean the teaching that some of the moral directives of the bible bind for all times, places and circumstances. Take the ten commandments, the New Testament directive about adultery/divorce, Paul's list of sins. For example, 'He who leaves his wife and marries another commits adultery'. That is clear, authorities will say; there is no room for any doubt about its meaning and application. So they will say that adultery is intrinsically

evil, that is, always and in all circumstances. Note
especially that the Catholic Church in its comprehensive
document on sexual ethics (1975) as well as in its
teaching on abortion (1995), the pastoral care of
homosexuals (1986), the indissolubility of marriage
(*Familiaris Consortio,* 1981) and the *Catechism of the
Catholic Church* (1992) appeals to specific biblical
passages or texts as *proof* of its position, so that you
often hear from church leaders that they cannot change
their official teaching. It is outside their control, they
say: it is *revealed*; and the primary source of that is the
bible, interpreted by the church.

I will cut to the chase here and say only that there
are considerable problems about such an appeal to
biblical directives. For one thing, the tradition down the
ages has found exceptions to them, as in the case of
killing, divorce, the status of women and of slaves. For
another, we find in the bible many different kinds of
directive and we blithely regard some of them – do not
swear, turn the other cheek, do not worry about
tomorrow, give to every one who asks – as ideals, as
important and commendable, but not *de rigueur.* But
why do we regard some directives as 'only' ideals and
others as strict rules. Might not divorce, for example, be
similarly regarded? Some theologians who have
suggested that have felt the wrath of authority. Further,
there are questions about the meaning of some of these
precise directives. About a timeless application of them:
when we talk about marriage or homosexuality today,

are we talking about the same thing as early Christians? There are questions too about the fact that some come from the ethic of the time (which, of course, is time-bound). That some are clearly culturally determined – for example, the biblical position on slaves and on women. That, in any case, the bible has its own diversity of positions: Paul's teaching in First Corinthians, the so-called Pauline Privilege, modifies the strict teaching on divorce. To reject an appeal to the biblical directives is not to say that such moral positions are wrong. It is to say that to accept them without question, solely on the strength of their being in the bible, is not valid.

Why would we need or heed such a moral revelation, anyway? Not many think nowadays that what is right and wrong actually depends on God's will, that God is actually making things right and wrong. But while they accept that it may not depend on God, many believe that there are problems in coming to *know* the truth. Some believe that we are not very good at working things out and that therefore we absolutely need God's guidance, a *revelation* of morality. So, 'it says in the bible'. Others refuse this kind of authority to the bible: they believe that, while it will have a generally formative effect in our lives, we cannot accept that its directives are of themselves decisive: we need just as much to use our intelligence to figure things out. So that, notwith-standing biblical directives, you have the debate among Christians about how to come to good judgment about marriage, divorce, homosexual acts etc. To put it crudely, how much do you depend on native moral sense and how much on the authority of the bible? Or how do you combine them? (It is a quandary today not only for Christian but for Jewish and Muslim interpreters of their holy books.) An important consequence for the public sphere is this: if Christians depend on a revelation for their morality, what hope is there for an agreement between Christian morality and that of humanist or other religious traditions?

Appeal to Natural Law ... But Clarified

Some Christian churches don't worry about this last point. They rejoice in difference: they will not have any truck with what they regard as secular or humanist morality. They expect to have a different take from others on moral questions. They are unapologetic about this. They maintain that their Christian tradition, with its language and culture, provides a framework that shapes the way those who have learned it perceive reality and order their lives. This means that an appreciation of the truth of Christian moral claims requires a facility with its entire world-view and only makes sense within that world-view. By contrast, the Catholic tradition, which is what I know best, expects considerable coincidence with the best of secular morality. It claims that many of its basic moral positions are matters of natural law. For example, its position about abortion, or contraception, or euthanasia, or homosexual acts, or divorce, or stem cell research, or cloning, or genetic engineering, or hybrid embryos. If it is a matter of natural law, that means that it is available to any right thinking person and must defend itself at the bar of reason.

But the Catholic position has a second card to play. It appeals to revelation for supporting argument. Its official position is that we are pretty good at working out the moral way, but that for clarity and certainty we need to have recourse to the bible. So it often appeals to the bible, interpreted by the church, to copperfasten its basic positions. For many people, this seems like a retreat into some kind of ghetto or esoteric morality, into an appeal to privileged information. Into an abandonment of rational debate in favour of submission to the divine decrees of the bible. But the orthodox Catholic position is that, when it does appeal in this fashion to revelation – whatever doubts theologians might have about the legitimacy of that – what it finds revealed there is the 'rational order', merely the fullness of the natural law. If people could see fully and clearly, it seems to say, this is the morality they would discover. So it sees its teaching as valid for all peoples and sometimes berates those who disagree with it, accusing them, for example, of failing to recognise human rights – it sees itself 'calling men back to the observance of norms of the natural law'.[1] There is a puzzle here. If it is a matter of natural law, of reason, or of human rights, why is it that there is such a divide between the

1. *Humanae Vitae* 11.

churches, particularly the Catholic Church, and that of much of society? How come so many intelligent and well-meaning people in philosophy, politics and medicine disagree with it?

A More Indirect Way to Rules: Ethos

We have already identified in paragraphs two and three (a) the general, open-textured orientations, and (b) the blunt appeal to biblical texts to prove the immorality of, say, divorce or same-sex relations. I wonder am I right in thinking that we need to explore another – weaker, less direct – form of appeal to the bible. (c) An approach to the bible that issues not just in the general orientations of (i) about poverty etc., which can be responded to in different ways, that does not (ii) make direct appeal to specific biblical proof-texts but that, nevertheless, leads to definite rules and to claims of natural law. Perhaps this looks complicated. But take, for example, the line of argument in *Humanae Vitae*: it appears to make an appeal of a weaker kind: its teaching purports to be 'founded on the natural law, *illuminated* and *enriched* by divine revelation'.[2] It is not appealing here to a particular text; its argument seems to be that the general spirit or outlook of the bible leads you to arrive at this conclusion.

As we wonder about the validity of that, it is helpful to consider that there are all sorts of reasons why people

2. Ibid., 4 (italics added).

differ in moral judgment. Background, temperament and philosophical world-view have an influence. Rationality presents itself differently in different cultural contexts: one person's rationality is another's naiveté. Many factors, often unconscious, go into a particular point of view. Could it be, then, that it is the religious ethos that makes the difference, even in what purports to be a natural law argument: could it be that one may expect the Christian world-view to suggest, in an indirect way, judgments about basic moral right and wrong. It seems so. I could put the question in another way: what is meant by Christian, or Catholic medical ethics, or life ethics, or business ethics? Crudely taken, it may mean just what the churches have taught. But I think that theologians who use the term want it to mean something more than that. Could it be that a Christian, or Catholic, or Buddhist, or Hindu, world-view leads you to specific moral conclusions – apart from any direct appeal to the ethical texts of its religious books? This raises a question about the very meaning of natural law. Can it be a matter of pure reason. Can it have the universal appeal that is claimed for it? Or is it always and necessarily coloured by philosophical or religious world-view?

Here are instances of that ethos, statements often found in Catholic morality: they are belief-statements or outlook-statements. Think how these might influence a person's perception and judgment. 'God alone is the Lord of life from its beginning until its end ...';[3] 'Called

3. *Catechism of the Catholic Church*, Dublin, 1994, 2258–80.

116

to give life, spouses share in the creative power and fatherhood of God';[4] 'God destined the earth and all it contains for all people and nations';[5] 'God entrusted the earth and its resources to the common stewardship of mankind';[6] 'All human beings, from their mother's womb, belong to God';[7] 'The environment is God's gift to everyone.'[8]

These are not exactly moral statements but they are a perspective. People who are part of this world-view are likely to have a particular point of view when it comes to issues of life, personhood, death, procreation, marriage. They are likely to see such matters as under the sovereignty of God and they will be tentative about taking any kind of freedom around them. (Only yesterday I heard an Anglican bishop on the radio use this very argument of 'life as a gift from God' to prove the immorality of assisted suicide.) This will not be the view of those who regard life as at worst an evil, at best a dubious gift; or those who regard humans as total masters of their own lives and destinies; or those who see the environment as solely for the benefit of mankind; or those who regard sex as solely for pleasure; or those who see economic life as a matter solely of and for the markets. Both sides might claim to be operating from reason or natural law, and Catholic authorities might say, as they say also about direct appeal to the

4. *Catechism* 2367.
5. *The Church in the Modern World*, 1971, 69.
6. *Catechism* 2402.
7. *Evangelium Vitae* 61.
8. *Caritas in Veritate* 48.

bible, that the religious viewpoint merely clarifies the human situation. But will they not come to different conclusions? It depends on where you are coming from, on the premises from which you start.[9]

(That Christian moralists disagree among themselves on the weight to be given to some general biblical orientations does not take from the fact that they agree in principle that such biblical thrusts should affect moral judgment. Their difference is about the interpretation of the bible, about the priority which they give to different biblical themes. There are well-known examples of theological tension in medical matters between those who see human creativity as a gift from God to be used in medical experimentation for the good of future generations, and those who have an absolute conviction that, because of God's covenant with each individual, one should not experiment on an individual for the sake of medical advance. Likewise, there is the well-known debate in South Africa and elsewhere between those who appeal to the contrasting biblical themes of conquest and liberation.)

So that even if we dismiss as dubious the direct appeal to universal and permanent biblical *rules* of conduct, the faithful adherence to biblical *stories* and

9. The remark of Alan Donagan is interesting, that 'the moral tradition associated with the Jewish and Christian religions is incompatible in various respects with other venerable moral traditions, for example that of Hinduism'. *The Theory of Morality*, Chicago, 1977, xv.

themes may lead to crucially different moral stances of
a substantive kind. So that what appears as natural law
is reason coloured by religious adherence. Is this the
traditional 'reason informed by faith' or what has been
called a 'faith-instinct' in moral matters – *Humanae
Vitae*'s 'founded on the natural law illuminated and
enriched by divine revelation'? If it is, it has to be
recognised as such. Difference is therefore to be
expected. If there is such a thing as Catholic medical or
sexual ethics, I take it that this is the provenance of it.
This does not mean that the positions arrived at are not
wise or humanly best. Nor does it mean that they will
not be shared by other religions and some non-religious.
They are far from being eccentric. There is nothing very
eccentric about belief in and commitment, at least in
broad terms, to the goodness of creation, of life and of
human community. But if Catholics feel justified in
taking this line of argument, two points might be
remembered. The first is that there must be recognition
that their viewpoints, and particularly concrete norms
too sharply drawn from them, will not necessarily
commend themselves to other sincere seekers of the
truth. The second is the danger that the approach will
be sloppy and that the hard slog of moral argument will
be bypassed. Even fellow-Christians may well argue that
inferences drawn from these premises are unwarranted.
For example, what exactly follows from the contention
that God is the author and lord of life? It does not
invalidate human creativity. Even the long tradition of

church teaching has had to wrestle with the question of when life may be legitimately taken.

A Christian Morality?

Is there then a specific Christian or Catholic morality? I take that to mean this: are there moral positions which commend themselves to Christians because of their particular faith-stance, but which do not appear justified to those who do not share that stance. For example, is it the case that a Christian understanding of marriage in some way entails norms that do not commend themselves to others, about divorce or contraception, for example? All in all, the question of a specific morality is not the most important question for Christians. What matters is to let the great thrusts of the bible influence us, without worrying about how specific it is. To be faithful to that ethos. That does not require any apology. But the question is important for other reasons – for inter-religious dialogue and for the public debate. An adequate discussion of this much debated and difficult question would take us far afield.[10] I say only this. It seems to me that every religion has its specific morality, one influenced by its outlook. The likelihood of agreement with others will depend on the term of comparison: some religions and world-views show considerable overlap, others do not. Many religions and

10. See Vincent MacNamara, *Faith and Ethics*, Dublin and Washington, 1985, passim.

philosophies, as efforts for a world ethic have shown and as we have seen in earlier chapters, espouse the broad moral claims of respect, justice and benevolence but may well differ in specifics.

There is another interesting angle to this. Even when people agree on moral action, they may still have a different morality. Take this as an example. Much theological thinking about the issue of the environment heavily invokes biblical themes of creation, covenant, stewardship, Sabbath, or the eighth chapter of Romans. What the theological appeal is doing in the argument is worth determining. It may be put forward as the basic source, the justifying reason of the argument, i.e. why it is regarded as morally good. Or as a further dimension to it, or as additional motivation for it. Or as a more complete context for it. Other religions or non-religious may be equally concerned about the environment for reasons innocent of and unconvinced by theology. For example, they see respect for it as a matter of moral obligation to future generations, or as a matter of natural humility before the mystery of the cosmos. Most likely, in the Christian view there will be a variety of reasons. But it is useful to know the logic of our position. Which may be particularly instructive, given the way biblical themes come in and out of favour – whatever happened to the rampant theologies of progress and hope of the 1950s and 1960s? Not only are they without advocates today but they seem to be discredited and regarded as wayward.

Why Are We Moral?

This leads neatly to one last question. Behind some of the criticism of religious morality is this issue: why are we moral? It is a justifiable concern. I have said in the first chapter that those who subscribe to the moral point of view do so for a reason – and that there are in the history of ethics several related justifications given for being moral, or theories of morality. Moralists may and do disagree about their foundational theories. But what there will be agreement about is that the fundamental reason for being moral is a reason from within the area of morality. The appeal of the teacher or reformer or society will be a moral one – the injunctions not to kill, or exploit, or cheat, or corrupt, or neglect the other, will be justified in terms of rationality, or respect, or fairness, or benevolence, or rights, or some such. Again, it is an appeal to the human spirit.

What this is leading up to is the contention that the moral claim should not be short-circuited by immediately attaching it to religion. To think of morality or the moral claim predominantly in terms of God at least runs the risk of devaluing it: it is possible for religion to do a disservice to morality. It is a failure here that has led to the jibe that religious morality is infantile. The great moralists have warned us: 'steady attention alone to so important an interest as that of eternal salvation is apt to extinguish the benevolent affections, and beget a narrow, contracted selfishness' (Hume); fear of God's will 'would inevitably form the basis of a moral system which would be in direct opposition to morality'(Kant): 'He therefore who avoids evil not because it is evil but because of the command of God is not free, but he who avoids evil because it is evil is free' (Aquinas). Performing what look like moral acts simply out of fear of God or fear of punishment hardly qualifies for morality at all. It may be an early stage of moral development, and anything that prevents murder or corruption or exploitation is not to be scorned. But there is a long way to go to true morality. It is important that religion should not delay the journey.

This is not to back off the position that Christians must do their morality in the light of their God-story and that this will colour their perception of what morality demands of them: the Christian story in fact enhances one's view of the inalienable value of the other. But it is to say that for them – as for other religions – there are different reasons for being moral. There are moral reasons, i.e. reasons which arise out of the kind of consideration just mentioned. These are central to morality, all morality, including Christian morality. They are what morality is about. There are also religious reasons, e.g. because it is the will of God, or to imitate God, or as an act of love of God, or to bring about God's plan or purposes or reign. Both kinds of reason are good. But to be moral solely for (religious) reasons extrinsic to morality, in particular the baser reason of fear, appears to lack true awareness of the human claim that is morality. It has long been a *dictum* of the Catholic tradition that grace does not destroy but builds on nature. If so, it respects what is one of the deepest human traits, its native moral awareness.

The earlier chapters considered the depth of our native moral thrust but also the fears, insecurities and urges that inhibit us from wanting to see the truth, and wanting to do it even when we see. To buy into the Christian vision is to enter a tradition and culture that is realistic about both those great strands of the moral journey. I think it is a defensible position that Christianity enriches moral life. To take the bible seriously is not to abandon one's native moral spirit. True, an unholy rage for order and discipline has led some churches into narrowness and inflexibility. True, there have been aberrations down the ages that have skewed the notion of morality, that have diminished the autonomy of the person, and that have distorted even the concept of God. You cannot deny that. But Christian morality is ever so much wider than official church statements or practice. Its spirit survives and is always seeking to re-emerge. Its core is that of all genuine morality – the centrality of the person. If that basic insight is suffused with Christian considerations, that is all to the good. There is room for a deepening and rounding out of our vision. Christianity helps that. It has its heroes and heroines, perhaps far from the centres of power, quiet, devoted, inspired by the tender goodness of God, the humanising mission of Christ, the action of the Spirit. They witness to its care for the human – even to the advocacy stance of its biblical tradition for the weak and marginalised. You would expect Christians to be to the forefront of causes for the liberation of humanity. Often, they have been.[11]

11. The Pontifical Biblical Commission recently (2008) issued a document, 'The Bible and Morality: Biblical Roots of Christian Conduct', which gives a striking overall view of the place of morality in Christian life. It acknowledges the problems about the use of the Bible in moral decision-making and offers excellent criteria for a credible approach. It rightly describes its own document as 'a breath of fresh air'. The Commission is, technically, an advisory body and its members insist that they are not moralists, but one expects that its work will be reflected in future official teaching.

CHAPTER 8
The Greatest of These is Love

Whatever approach you take to morality, it is clear that, as it is generally understood, it arises out of our being with others. It is not about impersonal or inexplicable rules or commands. Or if one can make any sense of the notion of a moral command, such as the Decalogue, they are commands about persons, ourselves included, doing them good or harm. So we find people variously saying that being moral is best understood as being loving, or respecting others, or acknowledging their human nature, or recognising their rights or their autonomy, or being impartial, or doing to others as we would have them do to us, or doing the actions that bring about the greatest amount of good for all concerned. Different ways of understanding our relationship with others, but all of them somehow recognising the centrality of the person. Such recognition of the significance of the other resonates fully with the Christian tradition. If one were to find a common thread or theme in the great variety of biblical morality, if one were to look for its most general orientation, respect for or love for the other would be a prime candidate. It is impossible seriously to subscribe to the Christian story, to celebrate the Christian memory, or engage in the praxis of the Christian community, without experiencing the overarching demand of love for others. All Christian traditions agree on that.

The Bible and Agape

The New Testament teaching appears to envisage a circle of love in which God's love is given to us and is to issue in love. This gives the Christian an identity: one belongs to a community that has its origin in love and that is directed towards love. Christians are to align themselves with the energy of that love: they have a mission towards the loving reign of God. That reign envisages the humanisation of the world, the overcoming of the obstacles to love, in our own hearts but particularly in the structures that are unloving – sin in and of the world. This is not to say that such concern is specific to Christians or that one needs to be a Christian in order to live a life of respect for others. We all know that non-Christians love their fellow human beings – indeed some may well claim that their love is more genuine than the love of religious people. But, as Christians see it, all love, wherever and by whomsoever it is lived, is from God, and all loving is a movement towards God. To be in love is to be in God. Let us look more closely at how the tradition sees it.

The word for love that is predominantly used in the bible is 'agape'. This was to become the distinctive expression for Christian love over against other expressions of love. There seems to be room for two interpretations of its essence. Some regard it as pure bestowal, sovereign, unmotivated save by the necessity to be itself, without any dependence even on the intrinsic worth of the other – in the likeness of God whose love, it is said, is sheer graciousness (*bonum est sui diffusivum*). Others include at least some element of appraisal: the other is to be loved because of the human being's intrinsic worth, perhaps additionally worth as a being from God and for God. The most obvious source of the love-teaching is the double commandment in Matthew 22:39, Mark 12:31, and Luke 10:27. But the belief that agape should characterise the Christian life does not depend on a command of Jesus. Nor is the teaching necessarily tied to the actual incidence of the word 'agape'. In Paul it is the whole kerygma that forms the basis of the demand, i.e. the whole story of the loving initiative of God in our regard. Agape-love is seen as a response to the very nature of God in his redemptive activity: it arises out of gratitude for God's grace; it is a gift of the Spirit; it should be – especially forgiving love – the attitude of one who has been forgiven by God. (cf. Rom 3:21; 2 Cor 4:4 and 5:14; Gal 4:4; Col 3:13). This inner dynamic of love appears all over the place (cf. 1 Jn 4:10-11, 3:16; Mt 5:44; Lk 6:27, 35).

New Testament love is active. It is true that in the Johannine literature it refers more to the community of the disciples: there it is a sign of true knowledge of God and of belonging to the community of light, a continuation of the love of the Father for the Son and of the Son for his disciples, a sign of credibility for the church. The Synoptic vision is wider: love is for all, even strangers and enemies, strikingly set forth in the Good Samaritan parable. We are to bless those who revile us and pray for our persecutors. We are to give without seeking a return, and not just favour those who favour us. In Paul it is not only active: it is the way of the imitation of Christ; it sums up the Christian life; it makes possible the resolution of conflicts and differences. There can be no doubting its centrality and significance.

Definitions: Regard and Commitment
There are few words that have such a wide range of applications as the word 'love'. I am interested here only in sketching the bare structure of love as a moral stance. When we talk morality, when we listen to our tradition of love, Christian or not, we are talking about relationship to persons, centrally if not exclusively. We live in a bewildering variety of those relationships – friend, spouse, lover, neighbour, parent, child, colleague, employer, employee, companion, fellow inhabitant of

this earth. They all have their own form, tone and demand. The moral tradition suggests that, in the rough and tumble of our living, while each kind of relationship has its own character, one word can cover all of them: love is the fundamental stance towards all.

But because it is such a vague and general word, much work has gone into sorting out the different shades and nuances of relationships that might pass as love. The medievals spoke of the love of desire, the love of benevolence, and the love of friendship. C.S. Lewis distinguished need-love and gift-love and identified four experiences: affection, friendship, eros and charity. There has been a considerable literature on the distinction between *agape* (regarded as an unselfish love of others in the likeness of God's love), *eros* (which has tended to be associated with desire and satisfaction and particularly sexual/erotic desire), and *philia* (friendship). We are all aware of the complexity and subtlety of our experiences of relatedness: it may be that the terms and concepts we have do not do justice to their variety; their light and shade emerge best, perhaps, in literature, with its sensitivity to the inner fugue of our thoughts and feelings. We do recognise, however, that one can, roughly speaking, distinguish between relationships that are predominantly self-centred and those that are predominantly other-centred. Of course, our motives and dispositions are usually mixed and we often cannot determine the exact mixture of selfishness and unselfishness. We often do not know our own hearts –

'strangers to ourselves, errant at the gates of our own psyche'.[1]

What does this moral stance of love mean in practice? Can we fill it out a bit? I go back to Gene Outka's well-known book on love. 'Agape is a regard for the neighbour which in crucial respects is independent and unalterable. To these features there is a corollary: the regard is for every person qua human existent, to be distinguished from those special traits, actions etc. which distinguish particular personalities from each other ... One ought to be committed to the other's well-being independently and unalterably; and to view the other as irreducibly valuable prior to his doing anything in particular.'[2] That is pretty general but I think it is fair enough. One can readily see the central importance of the triad of terms, 'human existent', 'irreducibly valuable', 'independent and unalterable'. All easily said. But we are here at the point of what is most deeply significant for us as human beings, what is at the heart of our civilisations.

Regard
There are two key elements here – regard and commitment. Commitment to the other's well-being will occupy me shortly. Let us look at 'regard' first. 'Regard' says

1. George Steiner, *Real Presences*, London, 1989, 139.
2. Gene Outka, *Agape: an Ethical Analysis*, New Haven and London, 1972, 9.

something about attitude or disposition towards the other. Minimally it points to a respect for the other. It is, I suppose, compatible with a certain natural antipathy. There are some people whom we naturally like and others with whom, for a great variety of reasons – to do with them and to do with us – and often at first sight, we do not experience any natural sympathy. We can hope to be able to reduce the number in this last category – and that is indeed possible – but we will hardly be able to eliminate it completely. We must still try to love all. Whatever about pure bestowal, love appears to require of us an appreciation of every other, some sense of reverence based on the fact of his/her being a human being, some sisterly or brotherly feeling. It requires that we appreciate at least the obvious fact of a common humanity and refuse to ignore it, whatever the temptations, whatever the natural antipathy, allowing it to make its claim on us. This regard or sympathy has a natural concomitant in action but it is not yet action. It refers to something that comes before action, that will accompany and issue in action.

To recognise and live this is the heart and heft of human life, what in earlier chapters I called authentic life, true life. This is listening to one's soul – this is what it comes down to. It is the central life-issue for us, the central moral and religious problem. This sense of the sacredness of every other is one of the most remarkable manifestations of the human spirit. In every age it throws up extraordinarily brave champions and witnesses. Most strikingly, it makes its claim in the universal recognition of – if not always respect for human rights, which gives some hope of being remembered even to the most downtrodden and persecuted.

> Even now there are places where a thought might grow –
> Peruvian mines, worked out and abandoned
> To a slow clock of condensation ...
> A thousand mushrooms crowd to a keyhole ...
> They are begging us, you see, in their wordless way,
> To do something, to speak on their behalf
> Or at least not to close the door again.
> Lost people of Treblinka and Pompeii![3]

Is there something mysterious about it? Not every philosopher will agree entirely with the following quotation but it struck me as worth quoting.

> It is deeply unnatural to reason to affirm that no human being, however evil their deeds and however foul their character, should be denied our unconditional respect, or be treated as though they are filth, having forfeited all right to justice. And it is even more deeply unnatural to affirm that people in severe and ineradicable affliction, who appear to have lost all that gives life meaning, should be fully

3. Derek Mahon, 'A Disused Shed in Co. Wexford'.

> our moral equals ... The need to affirm what reason
> finds offensive makes me speak of mystery ... I mean
> by mystery something which no powers of
> understanding can penetrate.[4]

There are those who say that it is only a religious – or
some analogous – realisation that each human being,
however apparently diminished, is created and loved by
God, that makes some kind of sense of this mystery, if
it be a mystery. Whatever about that, there can be no
doubt but that the religious, certainly the Christian
vision, powerfully underwrites the inalienably precious
character of each one and their imprescriptible rights.

We all, I suppose, pay lip-service to this. But living it
is a different matter. It is difficult because our hopes
and fears and needs are hopelessly intertwined with
others. Our selfhood depends on their regard, so that
the fate (self-esteem) of each of us is tied up with the
fate of others. We have no existence without others. We
are utterly reliant on them, mutually vulnerable. There
is no morality but in relation to them. It is here that we
succeed or fail as human beings. But, for all our
interlocking, it is incredibly hard to make ourselves
believe that others really exist in the same way that we
do ourselves, to accept that they exist for themselves
with similar desires and hopes and a similar destiny.

4. Raimond Gaita, *A Common Humanity*, London and New York, 1998,
38.

Even to treat them equally and impartially with ourselves, even to treat one other justly, is difficult. To go beyond it to positive regard, not just in our better moments, but as a settled disposition, asks a lot.

It is often pithily put by moralists that what is asked of us is to allow the other to *be other* – that is to recognise their independence and inviolability, to regard them always as an end and never merely as a means. But that is so difficult for humankind. Our best intentions can be sabotaged by ourselves, by a fifth column within us. So much depends on who we are who come to any relationship. What baggage of life's journey do we bring, what fears, what needs, what old patterns, what openness? It is a piece of Eastern wisdom that where there are others there is dread. Unconscious needs and fears about bonding, possession, survival and significance can easily betray us. The result is that we seldom really see the other. We see through the haze of our fantasies in relation to them. To give real assent to others, to rise out of our needs, is perhaps too much for human nature. This is not just about psychology or, if it is, it is where psychology meets and gives real, everyday content to morality. It is this that is the stuff of our lives. This is where I see the critical questions – about the problem, the possibility, and the direction of the moral response.

Commitment
Let us look at the second element in Outka's description of love as a moral stance – loving as bringing about the

well-being or welfare of the other. So love is related to doing. I take 'do' here in a very broad sense to cover the great variety of ways in which we affect one another. It will mean not only doing something but, at times, being silently supportive, staying with or suffering with another. Loving is to be judged by its effect on others. It is not merely a matter of what I, the agent, feel, of my intention, of the desire or emotion with which I do something. What happens to the other, or what I intend to happen is crucial. There are actions that cannot count as loving because of their effect on the other – however I feel or talk or protest about love. I may say that I meant something as an act of love, or intended it as such, or that I did it out of love. That – if it is genuine – is important and is obviously different from an act that is done out of hatred, envy or other evil intent. But it is not enough.

It is difficult at times to determine what are the ways or acts of love: do you spare the rod and spoil the child? And what is this 'tough love' they talk about? What I am maintaining is that there are ways of love, that they can be brought under the notion of well-being or human good, and that we must exercise our minds and our hearts about them. What well-being or flourishing means is not always immediately obvious: we made the point earlier that there will be difference about that, particularly of a cultural kind, and that we cannot expect to have knock-down proofs about differences. And because each of us is unique, with our very particular needs and fears and wounds, discovering what loving you calls for will require sensitivity, imagination and intuition from me.

Yet there is a broad fundamental structure of well-being, a basic cluster of needs, that is valid even from person to person, from age to age, from culture to culture. It cannot be loving wantonly to injure or diminish or exploit or corrupt, to deny health or education to others, to humiliate them, to keep them in dehumanising conditions – to do so is unintelligible to any elementary account of the human condition. There must be things that count as unloving, as well as loving. That is why 'all you need is love' will not do. We might perhaps regard this as painfully obvious were it not for the fact that there have been theological movements, especially in the 1960s, which mirrored the 'all you need is love' theme of the culture of the time. There developed a movement called Situation Ethics. It had two poles: the first, that all situations are different and so you could not have rules, so that what might be loving for me would not necessarily be so for you; the second, that all that matters in morality is to be loving. The movement was well-intentioned and sought to deliver us from a slavery to legalism, and it had important insights. But what it meant by love was slippery – was it to act *in* love, *with* love, *for* love, *with a feeling of* love? The result was confusion. It simply ignored the structure of the person. You cannot get away from the essentials of human existence.

We easily fail both in loving and in the love we expect. Take the difficult question of how love relates to desire. You don't love me just by meeting my current desires. Nor do I necessarily love you by meeting yours. And I don't love myself if I am simply led by my own desires. We have such a noisy plethora of desires. Perhaps it is best caught in our admission from time to time that we eat or drink or smoke or give way to self-pity *more than is good for us*, or that we have addictions of one kind or another. We need a system of priorities and we are born equipped to form one: wise living is about aligning ourselves with it. For long ages, philosophers have mused sadly over the fact that we act only when we see something as a good for us, as a value, something worth being or having, something that will satisfy us, but that often we delude ourselves about what is our real good.[5] The pursuit of current desires – or colluding with them – may well be appropriate. But they are not decisive. It is good for any of us to receive affirmation, esteem and healthy food – all of which we may well desire. It is good for us to be just and sober, to give up destructive relationships, to abandon corroding jealousies, to look after our health and spiritual well-being, to be fair to other sections of society, even though perhaps we do not currently desire any of these things,

5. One of the most famous remarks in philosophy is that of Socrates who said that no one does wrong willingly: he did not mean it as an excuse, but as part of his attempt to get people to see what was the true good and so avoid wickedness.

and, as we feel just now, could not imagine ourselves desiring them. In our hearts we know the truth about living: there is a sense of an inner good about it, but we don't always listen. We come back to the issue of the conversion of our minds and hearts, to the need for a deeper consciousness or enlightenment about the human condition. About what our interests actually are – and those of others.

Whether it is in giving or receiving, we have a problem with emotional maturity. Can we learn the difference, can we be guided by the difference, between what we desire – and therefore may try to seduce others into giving us – and what is truly worthy of our choice? On the other hand, are we able to be clear-headed about what those we dearly love crave from us, and what is worthy of their choice? Do we have the freedom – freedom from emotional neediness – which will enable us truly to give love and to receive love? Perhaps this is the key question of human development and moral life. If we cannot, we cannot. We can only hope to grow, and those who love us can do so best by helping us to face the facts more bravely, to see the truth about ourselves and our desires, gradually to unmask for us the rat-runs of our fantasies. Loving others is not just the task of valuing them and looking to their needs. We find that it involves us in a struggle with our own needs around them. It is only if we get some kind of freedom there that we are in a clear-eyed position truly to care. For Christianity, as for other traditions, it is this genuine response to the unconditionality of the other that makes for human wholeness. It sees this as the fulfilment of one's own being. This, it says, is where happiness, salvation, liberation occur. We are not constructed to be happy in selfishness.

CHAPTER 9
The Centrality of the Person:
Implications

In the last chapter we saw that recognition of the sacredness of the other, with the regard and commitment which it implies, is the heart of morality. It is the ground of the great variety of moral demands with which we find ourselves confronted – the source and justification of justice, fairness, equality, rights, concern for the planet, and a respect for sexuality and life. This has not always been obvious. The earlier moral teaching of command and prohibition in Catholicism did not look like that. It was impersonal, it did not bother to explain itself, it was experienced as a cold legalism. So that it is worth reminding ourselves that the whole moral enterprise is about the well-being of ourselves and others. If there is a role for the churches in morality that is its justification: Schillebeeckx put it, that 'Jesus comes offering all men and women a wholeness of life'. If it didn't feel like that in the past, for well over half a century now, many theologians, retrieving an earlier tradition, have insistently promoted a morality centred on the person, a morality whose core and inspiration and meaning is love. The implication of that approach is that, if I propose something as moral, I am committed to showing that it is the way of respect or love, that it is good for human nature, for society. That has been a seismic shift. It has made possible an understanding of morality that makes sense to people, that is attractive to anyone who has a care for humanity, and that connects with deep human longing.

Showing that may not always be easy, because, as we saw, the notion of wholeness or flourishing is coloured by one's world-view, but also because moral agreement depends on a sensitive openness to what it means to be a human person in society. And your hearer may not always be in that space. But if I cannot make some shot at showing it I am not talking morality. It is hard to overestimate the importance of this understanding of morality. A lot of other stuff has masqueraded as the way of Christian holiness or spirituality. In the fog it was easy for the great granite virtues of truth and justice and respect and equality – the basis of our civilisation, the primary expressions of agape – to be missed. Could it be that it was this schizophrenia that made possible the shameful disparagement of poor, disadvantaged children in the care of those vowed to service of Christ?

The Political
You sometimes hear the criticism that this movement, which made agape central, failed to stress the more

political and social responsibilities of life. That may be.
If so, it was a shortcoming. There is no conflict between
cultivating respect for the other and efforts for alleviating
the distress of the world – the bringing about of the reign
of God. On the contrary: the serious problems of society
have their roots in selfishness. It is this, more than a lack
of projects and schemes, that is the worm at the heart of
our problems. It may sometimes pay to be beneficent,
but an enduring willingness to transform structures and
institutions will arise only out of a sense of the inviolability of the other. The question for the churches and
for the world is whether this sense can be enlivened and
channelled into world-wide effect. It is hard to see that
there will be a global change of economic and political
life without some inner transformation, which will bring
moral and spiritual values to bear on economic and civic
concerns. Christians believe that God is inexhaustible
generosity and that the story of the world is the story of
God's giftedness to us: 'This dynamic of charity, received
and given, is what gives rise to the Church's social
teaching'.[1] If agape is to be genuine, it necessarily
becomes political and social – social love, a civilisation
of love, as Pope John Paul II put it, or what Benedict XVI
calls the institutional, the political path of charity.

So love has to be thought about not solely in
individual relationships but in terms of a common good
– 'the sum total of social conditions which enable people

1. *Caritas in Veritate* 5.

143

either as groups or as individuals to reach their fulfilment more fully and more easily' – conditions of an economic, legal, cultural and environmental kind.[2] That is the call on us at home and abroad – in the causes and the people we support, in the sectional interests we pursue or refrain from pursuing, in the political programmes we endorse, in an awareness of how our financial dealings impinge on the lives of others, in the interest we take in the actual living conditions of our society. We live in societies that have deep and corrosive inequalities – of income, of power and influence, of educational opportunity, of information, of access to health services.

Now, too, we are more aware of the wider world, of our solidarity as earth-inhabitants, more starkly reminded of the poverty, homelessness and displacement that so much of the world lives in. But we have become aware, I think, that our early notions of development, however well-intentioned, were simplistic and often thoughtless, not very sensitive to the real needs of other cultures, too little aware of the different layers of development, too blind to the many levels and forms of poverty and unfreedom. Not really tuned into what a true and integral development of peoples might mean. Increasingly, too, it dawns upon us that if we claim to have a care for our fellow human beings and for future generations, our greatest fear – and our greatest responsibility – must be the endless pillaging of the

2. *The Church in the Modern World* 26.

world's resources and the disaster of climate change which so starkly threatens lives and cultures.

Recent events have shocked us into the realisation of how intricately economic life is spun, of how disastrously the action or inaction of government, developers, investors and bankers affects the life of everyone, locally and internationally. In the kind of complex life that now obtains, in which the individual is easily disadvantaged or crushed by the political and economic machine, the notions of law and contract are not any longer adequate to encompass moral obligation. Not, indeed, that contracts are necessarily just: many a struggling state has had bitter experience of their injustice: they have, in the words of Don Corleone in *The Godfather*, been made an offer by the super powers that they can't refuse – a cruel, destructive offer. But there is an obligation not only to those with whom we have contracts or legal obligations. Our manner of business, our financial dealings, have far-reaching effects. We can do injustice to those we have never seen or thought about. We have a wider moral responsibility than we might previously have adverted to. This is not to propose anything unusual – it is just that the massive globalisation of life brings new forms of old obligations. So only a wider concept of the common good, one that has a more all-embracing sense of our responsibilities for the other, will be adequate. Human beings, wherever and whoever they are, are persons worthy of respect, not objects to be used.

Pope Benedict XVI is among those who call for a new sense of political and economic justice. The Church, as he recognises, may not be able to offer technical solutions to economic life and there may be a number of possible strategies. What it can do most credibly is re-awaken spiritual energy among its adherents,[3] encourage a more political and world-wide agape, and outline the moral parameters within which economic life must be pursued. And, ideally, encourage a move towards intermediate principles of action which will seek to close the wide gap between general aspirations and the actual situations of injustice which enslave people.

Adam Smith insisted that it is not from the benevolence of the butcher, the brewer, or the baker, that we can expect our dinner, but from their regard to their own interest. The anxious hope of religious and non-religious leaders today is that we can do better, that there will emerge an economic system which will not exclude profit, but which people will see also as a means for achieving human and social needs – fortunately, there are successful examples of this. We might underestimate the human capacity for a genuine love-justice. There is a vast reservoir of goodwill, as we see in the extraordinary response to appeals in times of disaster. The hope must be that the unselfishness shown in such situations will translate into the daily business of political, social and economic life. We have seen how

3. *Deus Caritas Est* 28.

imagination colludes with goodness of heart in non-governmental organisations, and in the various networks, institutions and projects that labour for justice. We all know people who have devoted their lives to causes of international justice and development. We have seen how interest groups have an effect far beyond their homeland. We know that we now have a say in political and economic groupings that have the destiny of the less fortunate in their hands. A morality of love can only be a morality of the common good.

You sometimes meet resistance to the notion of a common good in the name of individual freedoms and personal rights. It is true that there are problems here – about cultures, about pluralism, and about different conceptions of the good life. There are worries too about a 'rights-culture' that has too little regard for the great virtues we need to be part of society. But, far from being antithetical to the common good, manifestos of rights might best be seen as a bare sketch of its demands. They have played an important part in the protection of the weak and vulnerable. True, they were born less out of the communitarian view of ancient philosophy and more out of that of the new republics – an understandable response to the privilege and power under which earlier generations suffered. They continue to be an important bulwark. It is in the interests of the common good to point out that rights cannot be just asserted – the word is too easily slung around. The notion of a human right is a moral concept. A right has to be argued for in the context of our-being-in-society. And it is the human condition that there may be a clash of rights. It is not genuine rights that are the problem today, but an individualism that is confused with it and that is deaf to the wider considerations of the whole body politic.

Love as a Virtue

The Adam Smith remark reminds us that we can perform beneficent acts towards others for a great variety of motives. Giving material help to persons in need will look like an act of love. But I can give such help for all sorts of reasons, not all of them worthy. (It is true that some of the world's most useful work is done for mixed motives and sometimes for bad motives, and our motives may well be hidden from us: if we arrive at a more transparent and equitable economic life that will be mightily welcome, whatever the motives.) Jung has warned us of the danger of projection, of using the catch-cries of justice to deny the evil in our own hearts, to boost our own virtue or moral superiority. The danger is that, whatever our good intentions, the energy we are putting into the atmosphere may be anger, self-righteousness, control and power: '... indignation comes to be fuelled by hatred for those who support and connive with these injustices, which in turn is fed by our sense of superiority that we are not like these instruments and accomplices of evil. Soon we are blinded to the havoc we wreak around us. Our picture of the world has safely located all evil outside of us.'[4] More laudably, I can act out of duty. I can give others what they need and what I may be in duty bound to give. It is something. It may be much. But one has some distance to go in order to act in love. Doing what is good for others is not necessarily loving them. *What* I did for others – my stance as a moral person – cannot be described without some attention to *why* I did it. Love is a virtue of attachment as well as of action and the disposition of the heart is part of the virtue. As some of the great spiritual traditions advise, it is those who have learned compassion in the heart who can show compassion.

But let us keep our feet on the ground. I cannot love the whole world – can I love anyone? – with the utterly outgoing and disinterested love of God. I can respect them for what they are as persons and hope gradually to enrich that with a loving disposition. Many of us would be very happy if we could manage that. There is a wide range both in the quality and the quantity of our response. There are also different urgencies. There will be more or less urgent calls on us. Philosophers are accustomed to distinguishing between 'rock-bottom duties' and supererogation or ideals: some of them drive a wedge between the two, so that ideals such as charity, benevolence, disinterested kindness and devotion to the service of others do not fall within the purlieu of

4. Charles Taylor, *A Catholic Modernity?*, New York, 1999, 33.

morality. Even the Catholic tradition has in the past distinguished duties and counsels of perfection – what appeared to be a morality for lay people and another for religious. That is hardly present-day thinking. Post-Vatican II moral theology recognises only one perfection: for it, Christ is the norm of a seamless morality. And yet we must beware of impossible ideals.

Self-Love

If agape is unselfish and disinterested love in the likeness of God, what of the niggling worry about desire: is there always a failure if our love is tainted with desire? In some theological writing it has been associated with selfishness. The notions of need love and gift love, and of *agape, eros* and *philia*, may be helpful but they are not decisive. Eros has had a bad press in Christianity – Nietzsche complained that Christianity had given Eros poison to drink – and some theologians have even worried that the delight of our restless hearts in God is a matter of selfishness. But eros, longing, desire, is one of the great thrusts of human life. From time immemorial, philosophers have spoken about our desire for and delight in beauty and truth and goodness. That is something that is God-given. There are base forms of selfishness in love of others: I can love them only for what I get out of it, and I am always in danger of sliding into that. But I can love someone who delights me and much of that love may be disinterested love. True, the relationship satisfies some basic longing. But such is humanly important. Normally such delight means that I affirm the other and wish the other's good: it is not just selfishness, although there is the ever-present danger that it might become just that; if I should cease to love when delight vanishes, that would be significant. Yeats, I think, had it right:

> I heard an old religious man
> But yesternight declare
> That he had found a text to prove
> That only God, my dear,
> Could love you for yourself alone
> And not your yellow hair.[5]

We have been skirting that old conundrum for moral theology, the question of self-love. The Christian tradition has gone through all sorts of contortions about it and there are many theories of what is meant by it. If agape, at least in one version, has to do with valuing and loving the human person because of intrinsic worth, it is hard to see why it would not mean valuing oneself and one's own flourishing. There is a love of oneself that does not deny or ignore the other. It is difficult truly to love oneself. It calls for an authenticity that is not a shallow self-satisfaction. It takes a lot of wisdom to realise what I most deeply want, and to be open to it. The wholeness of my being, what my nature as a whole

5. W.B. Yeats, 'For Anne Gregory'.

demands, encourages me to relativise my narrow desires, but its voice is often not welcome. So it is a life-long struggle and we may not have much to show. That said, however, a sense of autonomy, of strength, of delight in one's being and energies, is an elemental human need. Indeed it is only people who have a respect for themselves, who value themselves as persons, and who have attained a certain security within themselves who are in a position to be open to the unconditionality of the other. So that our own well-being facilitates the well-being of others, though this is not necessarily the only justification for it. Further, it is openness to the other that is the way of our own fulfilment as persons, our deepest satisfaction: it is, as we noted before, doing what we most want to do.

It is important to love out of strength, not out of weakness. Lack of a sense of self-worth is one of the most universal of human tragedies. The sense of scarcity, of wound, of deficiency, drives us, so often unconsciously, to do foolish things – to fawn, to flatter, to criticise, to envy, to bury ourselves, to love falsely. Psychologists and therapists are well aware of the internal chaos it causes. Strength allows us to be realistic: it enables us even to love our shadow. Women especially have had much to endure here. Centuries have put on them the role of sufferer and sacrificer, have praised submission and uncomplaining devotion as the way of love. But an unqualified call for the surrender of selfhood inhibits our becoming a person who can relate in love to God, to other people, to the world, and to our own emerging, fragile self. It is not only selfishness and possessiveness that are obstacles to the development of Christian love, but also the very lack of self.

Priorities

But to pick up a phrase from the second-last paragraph: what if our care for ourselves does injure others? Life does not come simply. It is the very human condition that needs and desires clash – ours and those of others. Choices in life often involve asking who is to be disadvantaged. And then what does love require of us – that we treat ourselves and others equally, prefer ourselves to others, prefer others to ourselves, forget ourselves, deny ourselves, in the interests of love? All those positions have been espoused and one could probably find support in scripture and in the Christian tradition for every one of them. Few texts have endured such a bruising as that which enjoins that we should love 'our neighbour as ourself'. Things become even more tricky when we add in another old conundrum, that of priorities: whom should we love first, those nearest to us (spouse, child, parent, sibling, friend, lover, fellow countrymen and women) or those in greatest need – the nearest or the neediest? Does charity begin at home? Or is it, as Paul tells us, that charity seeks not its own? Suppose it comes down to a choice between giving my children holidays, games, music, ponies, higher education, or using the resources involved to help others in great need, even those we will never meet? We can fail in love towards our fellow human beings by omission as well as by commission. There are those who think we may not allow ourselves or our special relationships anything but the necessities for a decent human life, while others are in dire need of and will be helped by our assistance.[6]

We can hardly deny our need for, and right to, special relationships of the kind mentioned. They too are part of being a normal human being: to have and to favour this friend or this partner is not a failure of love to others. It is a human right: I marry this man/woman rather than that. Indeed to enter such relationships, what the tradition called *philia* or friendship – mutual, unselfish, fulfilling – is sometimes proposed as the ideal expression of love. Yet there will be situations that make us think. There are multitudes that are denied the basic rights to food, clothing, and a home, and that is something that we can sometimes influence. But, in doing so, we can hardly simply ignore special relationships. It is not possible to give a formula here or to declare clear obligation. One cannot just baldly say, 'you may prefer yourself to others', or 'you should prefer the neediest to yourself'. Nor can one say, 'you may prefer your nearest and dearest to strangers', or 'you should prefer the neediest to your nearest'.

6. See Peter Singer, *The Life You Can Save*, New York, 2009.

The ideal of many traditions, Christian or not, appears to demand that we look to others' basic needs before our own lesser need, certainly to others' extreme need before our own luxuries. The fact that we know more about the world's problems today amplifies our moral obligations. We cannot close our eyes: we cannot let the starving die. To say that is to be vague, of course: 'needs', 'luxuries', 'superfluities' are slippery terms, and our special relationships are various. Much remains unresolved: does agape demand that I pare down my living style to what is absolutely necessary and give what remains to the suffering of the world? I don't think one can give a formula. We can only keep the issue vividly before us and favour a bias towards the neediest. Much depends on possibilities, on character, on how critical our particular intervention might be, and on the likely efficacy of our help.

When Christians are asked about their morality they answer spontaneously and rightly, even glibly, that it is a morality of love. But we have to find the ways of love. What that means may be much more complicated than immediately appears. The next chapter takes us into even deeper waters.

CHAPTER 10
Is Love All You Need?

It must give us pause that an eminent philosopher has said about a morality of love that, while it is widely advocated by Christians, its theological exponents are neither clear nor of one mind.[1] He is implying that when it comes to the test, to the nitty-gritty of particular decisions, it is too vague and won't do the job. We all, Christian or not, can go some distance in saying what morality requires of us. But the demands of living are sometimes complex and puzzling: test yourself with issues of stem cell research, spare embryos, drug trials, surrogate motherhood, sperm donation, rights to information, development projects, freedom of the press, cooperation of various kinds, pollution of the environment, embedded traditions of bribery. Sometimes a problem is not easy even to describe or to circumscribe. So how might we solve

1. William Frankena, *Ethics*, Englewood Cliffs, 1963, 42.

them? I think it is fair to say that to depend wholly on common sense or vague talk about love is not to be fully human: we deserve a more reflective life. We ought to be able to make some shot at how we arrived at the moral positions we hold; to be able, too, to recognise what is involved in the everyday debates of a moral and political kind. It won't do just to make assertions or to take refuge in 'well, that's how I feel' or 'that's what my church tells me', or 'I think it is all about love'. People won't be very impressed by that: they'll expect us to be able to give reasons.

Down the ages, philosophers and theologians have suggested decision-procedures that might serve us in our moral conundrums. These deserve a study in their own right and I intend to offer just that in this chapter, however briefly. This is difficult stuff, but it is a way of sorting out our moral convictions and intuitions, of figuring out what we believe and *why*. Otherwise you may find yourself stopped in your tracks by someone who says: 'what you say seems to imply that you would be prepared to sacrifice an innocent life if the situation were desperate enough'; or 'so you think what really matters in an act is whether the person meant well'; or 'so you think there are cast-iron rules that we must never violate'. Or whatever. All I am trying to do here is tease out implications of different positions. Among other things, it may also help us to find out what we mean by loving others. I suspect that, in practice, even those who espouse a morality of love need to enlist other principles to guide them. Love-talk tends to morph into some of the well-known moral theories, especially in the difficult cases when many are affected by acts, when it is a matter of who is to suffer. The nature of the problem – and the complaint of my philosopher – will be clearer when we have a look at different approaches to morality.

I note three well-known theories: (a) the virtue approach; (b) the approach which enjoins that we perform the act that brings about the greatest amount of good; (c) the approach which is stated in terms of rules. While all three are versions of how we are to relate to the human condition of being with others, their advocates are not necessarily interested in thinking of morality in terms of love – not everyone agrees that taking love as central is the most satisfactory approach to morality – but what they have to say is relevant to that. We mustn't think that they will always give us radically different solutions. The theories will often agree in practice about particular issues. Roughly speaking, you could say that some approaches lean more towards seeing moral life in terms of the kind of person one ought to be – and they tend to be maximalist – others on what one ought to do and particularly on what one ought to avoid – and they tend to be minimalist.

A. Virtue: Be A Good Person
Do you think we ought to consider moral life primarily as a matter of becoming a certain kind of person? Don't jump to the conclusion that this is narcissistic, that it

proposes a self-centred approach, or that it is not compatible with agape-love. Virtue ethics is based on the understanding that we are beings of a certain make-up, who have the possibility of developing and flourishing by a distinctive way of life in our societies. We share a broad range of needs with others in society and we are presented with the challenge to become the kind of person who will be a decent citizen, or as we sometimes say, a credit to society. The character we have formed will shape how we live: it will determine what we see as worth doing in life. It will facilitate the doing. It will affect how it is done. Virtue is not simply a matter of being – 'be honest, don't be dishonest'. It implies action – 'do what is honest, don't do what is dishonest', 'do what is the loving thing, don't do what is unloving'. A truly just person will know, for example, that just acts are to be done, will ideally know what acts are indeed just, and will have an inclination to do them – and to do them because they are just. There is implied a continuous growth in moral perception, in wisdom about life in society. Individual fulfilment and communal well-being are mutually supportive.

This is a very ancient way of looking at moral life and it is much in favour again. Its advocates say that this is how we should teach people about morals. So that, rather than just giving them rules about what to do and what to avoid, we should try to enlist their interest in truth, justice, fairness, honesty, fidelity and so on – the qualities which they might see as essential to a decent society. It is true that societies through the ages have a somewhat different vision of the human being and of what makes for a flourishing society: it is this vision that will indicate what virtues are appropriate and necessary. There will be a fair amount of agreement about this, and therefore a widely recognised range of virtues and vices. And yet, because societies differ in their understanding of the person and of human needs, because they are rooted in traditions and world-view, because they exist in material and social conditions, there will be differences from age to age and from place to place – between the virtues honoured in a Greek society of Homer's time and our society, between Western, Eastern and African society. There will still be analogies and overlap. It will still be possible to talk to one another, to dialogue across cultures about what a full human life means. We can and do, after all, sit down from time to time as a world community – think of all those international conferences – to discuss hunger, justice, rights, development, and to agree on common undertakings.

Remember that striking remark of Herbert McCabe that I referred to earlier. He said that being moral is doing what one most wants to do – what in our very best and truest moments we would somehow like to be. That, I suppose, is the challenge for all of us, and it is far from easy, given the difficulties with which we are beset. But the hope is that we can grow into wanting what is truly humanly desirable, more open to goodness, wiser in judgment, more content with a life of virtue. Morality is not exactly an acquired taste, but one can come to appreciate it more and allow it to take greater root in one's life. There is always the possibility of educating one's desires. So there are degrees of virtue. It is a whole life's journey: none of us will fully realise it. We will be at best very pale shadows of the ideal. It will be a matter of inching forward.

There is much to be said for this approach. (i) It does not limit moral life to particular points or precepts. It is an all-embracing vision, as is Christianity. It recognises the historical nature of life, how we form our character, how our past affects the present and opens up future possibilities. (ii) It is plastic, adapting itself to different societies and eras. (iii) It is interested not just in what we do but in our goodness as doer, not just in the doing of acts but in how they are done – they are to be done in the manner of the good person. It values inner life and offers a greater interiority to morals: it concerns itself with our reasons and motives. (iv) It aspires to the education of our desires, so that we will not only come to want what is truly good but find some joy in pursuing it. It was in such virtue-terms that the Greeks and the great medievals thought. Perhaps we too might think thus of moral life. Not as a set of rules but as an invitation to reach towards the fullness of being, towards an ideal of beauty in living. We might think of the mysterious moral 'ought' and of moral obligation as the inner call of our humanity, a call to our imagination, rather than as a law imposed on us. We would see our refusal, then, as a sad human failure – rather than as the violation of a law – as a failure to master the craft of being a human being. Such an approach seems to me to resonate with the great spiritual traditions and their wisdom.

B. You Should Do What Will Bring About The Greatest Good

It is hard to see that a rounded moral life would not incorporate some or all of these virtue-attitudes. I think all of us would aspire to them. And it has to be acknowledged that many moral systems, especially those of religious and spiritual provenance, whatever their core concern, do make room for something of this kind. (Thus, while many associate Christianity with rules and prohibitions, it has also held out to its followers the ideals of goodness, generosity, love and forgiveness, although there was difficulty in harmonising the two approaches.) It is often argued that an exclusively virtue approach is inadequate and lacks the spine of moral argument. Not everyone is happy that it is sufficient moral guidance to tell people to 'be forgiving' or to 'be loving' or 'to learn compassion' (or, analogously, to tell Christians to seek the reign of God). It may not help much to tell a surgeon to be loving, when he/she is faced with a newborn baby with severe defects, requiring difficult operations, and with a limited life expectancy. Or to tell the couple whom I saw on television the other night to be loving, when they agonised about what to do with spare embryos after successful IVF. What is 'being loving' to mean in practice?

Our virtue-wisdom is often not up to the complicated task when the interests of many are involved. Anyone who has reared a family knows what it is like to try to make decisions in the best interests of all. How do you do the moral thing? It sometimes looks as if, in some respects, one member has to be sacrificed to the other. But is that fair or just or caring? You often find yourself torn or conflicted, pulled two ways. Hidden in such domestic problems is a major issue of moral theory. You could depend on virtue, if you had become very wise, to bring you to the right judgment. Or do you need something else? There is a well-known theory that purports to address such a problem and thousands of problems like it, some small, some world-shattering. It says: you are morally obliged to perform the act that will bring about the greatest advantage to all affected by your act, including yourself. Knowingly to perform any other action is to take a morally wrong course.

This means that you do a kind of sum, adding everything up. Is this, in fact, what you do instinctively? I use the very general and vague word 'advantage'. What are you meant to add? How would you as a parent in the family situation come to a conclusion about what is best? There are several forms of the theory – which variously say that you add utility, or pleasure, or happiness, or people's preferences, or states of affairs including health, even certain moral qualities of all those affected by your act. There are problems about making any kind of calculation of this kind; indeed some think it is impossible. However, many Catholic theologians have embraced a form of the theory: they say that we are to do the act that will bring about the greatest good. They mean 'good' in the sense we referred to in chapters one and eight – what is good for you, what is your well-being. That, of course, is not simple either. Here is how one of them puts it: 'We must consider the moral rightness or wrongness of an act by considering all goods and evils in an act and evaluating whether the evil or the good for human beings is prevalent'; harm may be justified, they say, in terms of the whole act by the proportionately greater good.[2] Thus they are referred to as Proportionalists. (The notion of proportionate assessment is not foreign to official Catholic morality: you find it, for example, in teaching about the obligation to take means to preserve one's life and widely in canon law.)

Many moralists qualify the general theory in various ways, which I shall indicate in a moment, but the key point here is that the decision about the right act depends on the effect of your act – what will happen, what will be brought about – and that, of course, is sometimes unpredictable. But that is what you are

2. Josef Fuchs, *Christian Ethics in a Secular Arena*, Dublin and Washington, 1984, 82.

meant to keep your eye on. That is what matters. It is the sum of the effects that determines whether what you did was right or not: the means to the end – who suffers what, for example – are to be weighed but are not considered independently of the total result. Or as they sometimes put it – the right (act) depends on the good (on the amount of human good or value achieved). It may look abstruse. But I suspect that is often what people do quite instinctively. They'll say that they did what they thought was best, *all things considered.*

Think of government decisions – ours ultimately. Laws that limit your freedom to buy drink when and where you wish, to sell your goods as cheaply as you wish; that penalise you for using plastic bags or smoking in pubs; that insist on taking your money in income tax; that will compulsorily purchase your property; that will punish you for not wearing a seat-belt; that determines just who will receive free medical care; that bans or criminalises certain acts, programmes or behaviour; that decides whether to spend on social services, or on education, or culture, or infrastructure, or the recapital-isation of banks. There are a thousand examples. Presumably a politician would say that he/she is seeking the greatest good of the community, of all concerned. Or that he/she is doing what is the public good or in the public interest. Most of us go along with it most of the time, although in all cases some individuals or sections are sacrificed to others, and some people vociferously argue that their *good,* or their *rights,* or especially their *freedoms*, are being violated in this mass calculation. You hear it all the time.

But there is a downside to seeking the greatest good. You can easily think up situations that give you pause. What about this? You breach the moral obligation of confidentiality you have entered into with your client (who has Aids or is suicidal or homicidal) in order to prevent harm to others. You refuse to pay your debt to me saying that it will do greater good if given to the starving of the world. You ban Muslim headscarves or crucifixes in school in the interests of *laïcité*. You force-feed hunger strikers. You subject terrorist suspects to dehumanising conditions, or you introduce extensive and intrusive surveillance, or imprisonment without trial, or you give the police scope to bug private conversations – on the grounds of protecting the populace against terrorism. You use the body-parts of deceased children for valuable research, without reference to the family. You take cells from an embryo, which results in its death, in the hope of developing stem cells to alleviate the devastating effect of Parkinson's disease or spinal injuries. You shoot army deserters at dawn *pour encourager les autres*. You raze homes and schools in Gaza or Sri Lanka in order to clear out insurgents – for the overall good of the country. You drop a nuclear bomb on a Japanese city because it will end the war and ultimately save more lives. You seem to be violating people's rights or freedoms in various ways. You may argue that in the overall you are doing what is best.

The theory is seductive. It often takes the form of, 'Consider the enormous benefits if this is done, or consider the harms that will be avoided'. That is an important moral consideration, but it is not decisive and often comes with the innuendo that those who do not agree are lacking in human sympathy. It is the kind of remark you often hear from proponents of embryonic stem cell research or other medical experimentations: they point to anticipated benefits for those who are suffering. It is hard to disagree, and sometimes those who do so are reproached with the slur of only wanting to keep their hands clean in the messy and complex business of doing what is best for humankind. Can you really rely on the theory? Many say no. In its crude form, does it not go against our common moral convictions: it seems to subordinate people to an impersonal overall lump of utility or happiness and to condone killing, or lying, or injustice, or violation of individuals and their rights, if that results in greater overall good. Does it not also violate our sense of fairness or justice: we want, I think, to say that morality cannot be just a matter of the greatest overall utility or good; there should be something about the distribution of goods, about fairness, and some special consideration for the less well-off. These are moral concerns which we find valid independently of the consequences. We don't want them to be steamrolled in the name of some total calculus. They are the kind of considerations that reveal one's political philosophy. Does the common good coincide with the greatest sum or amount of good as understood from this perspective? Or does the common good require the enduring structure of rights and rules and special consideration for the less well-off? If you are listening at all to modern debates about medicine, life-issues, economics or politics, you need to have some stance about such matters.

It can be argued that the principle of the greatest good is made stronger and more acceptable if we take certain qualifying measures – and you find that Proportionalists are among those who insist on them. For example: (i) be sure to take full account in your calculations of the long-term harmful consequences for any society of, say, killing an innocent – could you ever justifiably overlook it? Or of limiting important freedoms. (ii) Look to rules rather than acts. So keeping promises, honouring contracts, paying debts, telling the truth, respecting life, are important for the well-being of a society: it is their observance that will bring about the greatest good, not because they will do so in a *particular instance*, but because greater good follows for society if they are generally followed. (iii) Be sure that your action does not undermine the very value you are protecting, as it would if you were to take an innocent life in order to protect the lives of many.

There are plenty of moralists – the majority perhaps – who regard the theory as perfectly adequate, especially if (i), (ii) and (iii) are factored in. Others formally suggest a mixed theory, supplementing the naked principle with other considerations. The general approach, they acknowledge, makes an important contribution to moral thought – it *is* desirable that we seek the greatest good – but it does not adequately cover the whole area of morality and needs to make room for considerations of the inviolability of the individual, for justice, fairness, basic rights, and the needs of the less well-off. The purists might argue that such considerations would in any event weigh heavily in their calculations. But for them it is still a matter of calculation of overall benefit. Those who opt for a mixed theory, and again Proportionalists are among them, want such matters to be given a strong, independent status and sometimes to overrule the benefit argument.

All this may be wearying and appear to make moral life unnecessarily complicated. There may be concern also that it drags us down and away from the great broad thrust of the Christian story, and of the morality which it adumbrates. Good people usually get things right without any advertence to theories. And yet one must see the value and, at times, the necessity of the analysis. Even within religious ethics you find authors leaning towards one theory or the other. The Vatican saw fit to issue an encyclical, *Veritatis Splendor* (1993) excoriating theologians who adopt a greatest good theory. Why? There is clearly an understandable concern for the inviolability of the individual. But there is also the fact that, in its most obvious form, the theory undermines the stance of the Catholic Church – and of others – that there are some acts that are intrinsically wrong and that

169

THE CALL TO BE HUMAN

no good consequences will justify. The stark version of the theory does not accept that there is any act – anything at all – that is absolutely and always wrong. In the end the right act or rule will be the one that brings about the greatest amount of good, however it does that. We'll have more about that in the next chapter.

C. There Are Rules Which Bind Us

There are those who will have no truck whatever with all this talk about bringing abut the greatest good. They say: I don't want to hear about consequences or outcomes; I don't need to know. For them the heart of morality is a set of rules that identify classes of acts that are right or wrong, obligatory or prohibited. They contend that there are features of some acts, other than their consequences, that make them right or wrong. And so there are standards independent of the end result for judging the means. It is wrong to kill another, they say. It is wrong to lie. It is wrong to sacrifice confidentiality. It is wrong to break promises or dishonour debts. It is wrong to have same-sex relations. Once you know that an act falls under this description or has this con-comitant, you can say that it is *prima facie* wrong: you don't need to take into account further consequences. So there are *rules* of right and wrong: such acts, some will agree, may not be always wrong – because there may be a clash of rules – but their wrongness is not a matter merely of consequences. Catholics are very familiar with this kind of thing.

Where do advocates of this theory find their rules: how do they justify them? Variously. Among the most common you find the claim, and we have seen problems about it, that God has revealed such a code of moral rules, as in the Decalogue or in the New Testament. Or the claim of natural law, in one or other of its formulations. You often hear that Catholic moral theology is based on natural law. But it is a mistake to see it solely as a Catholic theory: it has its roots in the very beginning of philosophy. It is the conviction that as rational beings we know that there is a moral way, that we recognise it as a demand on us, and that right action is in some way indicated by what we are, by what we call our human nature. The natural law theory is general and flexible. The most controversial version of it was one that held sway until recently. Its interpretation of human nature was the narrow one of the physical/biological structure of the person with its natural faculties and their obvious purposes or ends. These factual, physical orientations or 'laws', this version says, indicate what is *morally* right: it is moral to act in a way which respects their natural purpose or efficacy, immoral to frustrate them, to 'act against nature': 'the moral law obliges them in every case ... to respect the biological laws inscribed in their person'.[3] Here biology is the determinant: reason simply notes and submits to the biological lines. It is wrong to 'interfere' or 'frustrate'.

3. *Evangelium Vitae* 97.

This is largely discredited now. It could not deal with the question: why are biological laws elevated into being the moral law; by what reasoning are they given ethical significance? (Or why is so-called 'interfering' or 'frustrating' regarded as immoral rather than as a creative use of your intelligence for your well-being and perhaps that of others?) It ignored the psychological, social and cultural make-up of the person in society. A crucial test, of course, was the matter of contraception. Does intelligence mean obeying the biological processes of conception[4] or does it enjoin one to be creative in bringing about human flourishing – whatever about such processes? In particular, what justification is there for distinguishing so-called natural and artificial methods of contraception? The theory led to difficult conclusions and devious arguments in other areas also, for example, in the use of the faculty of speech and in some medical procedures. In religious circles it was underpinned by the world-view that God has created the world with all its laws and purposes, that these are his/her will for mankind, and that to 'interfere' is to disobey the divine ordinance. But how does one arrive at the assertion that this is the divine will?

You find that recent Vatican documents supplement their teaching with something wider than a biological approach: they support their rules by appeal to 'essential human and moral values which flow from the very truth

4. *Humanae Vitae* 16.

of the human being',[5] or to 'the ordered complex of "personal goods" which serve the "good of the person": the good which is the person himself and his perfection'.[6] Some of this echoes the position of an influential school of theologians. Their position is that the intelligent person grasps that certain human inclinations are values for us, or are humanly worthwhile: they list life, knowledge, play, aesthetic experience, friendship, practical reasonableness and religion.[7] The claim is that, since these are essential human goods, it is irrational and immoral to intend to destroy, damage, impede, or violate any of them, that is, ever to act directly against any one them. So, a contraceptive act is immoral because it is contrary to the good of life. All the goods are considered to be equally important, so that one can never yield to another. They are inviolable, absolute. It has to be said that this is not a form of natural law argument that all theologians find compelling. They do not accept that this is how reason functions, nor do they think that direct clashes of values can be avoided.

The broad basic principle that intelligent choice is related to what we are as human beings remains valid: to behave in a way that is destructive of the person goes against reason. What was required was an account of

5. *Evangelium Vitae* 97.
6. *Veritatis Splendor* 79, 48; cf. *Morality of Conjugal Life*, London, 1997, 16.

7. This is a very skeletal account of a substantial moral theory. See the various writings of John Finnis, Germain Grisez, Joseph Boyle, William May.

the human that takes seriously not just our physical/ biological but our psychological, social and cultural make-up – satisfactory human living and human dying. This calls for an awareness of the whole human condition and an experience in the living of it, a knowledge guided and supported by imagination, feelings and a full sensibility. Such a version of natural law based on our nature adequately considered makes sense. It admits of rules – although there will certainly be argument about how valid or universal such rules can be. I suggested earlier that different world-views about human nature may well lead to different conclusions (chapter seven). Likewise, an awareness of its historical character, of its complexity, and of the social construction of reality (chapter four) means that we will not call something natural or human or normal that is merely cultural or socially shaped. It renders suspect what was a central tenet of the traditional theory – that human nature is universal and unchanging, and that therefore one can cleanly deduce from it universally valid negative rules for all peoples in all times and cultures.[8]

Comment

So what of our different theories? Major questions about a rules approach will be considered in greater detail in the next chapter. I note here that it tends to be about negative norms, about the frontier of morality. So that it

8. *Sexual Ethics* 4, *Veritatis Splendor* 4, 52.

is a morality of what one is minimally obliged to do rather than about the fullness of moral life, about moral vision. On the other hand, the approach that says that it is immoral not to do the act that brings about the greatest amount of value – and we should remember the difficulty of calculating this – appears to be quite the opposite and puts an enormous burden on everyone: can we possibly be saddled with this in every decision? But, in fact, as I mentioned in an earlier chapter, moralists of this ilk quite explicitly hive off works of supererogation from the area of morality: more credibly they distinguish obligations of not harming and doing good. Both theories are left with a rather thin concept of moral life. Moreover, in both theories, moral argument is thought of purely as a guide to action. It is concerned with what it is right to do, rather than what it is good to be. That differs greatly from the virtue approach with its concerns about the why and the how of action, with the inner life, with the meaning of the human person, with the imagination of the good life. This is not to say that, in practice, either individuals or cultures limit their moral vision. It has been part not only of the religious but of the secular traditions to exalt generosity in life, and in general to hold out the way of virtue. The thrust of that, however, is to distinguish, perhaps too sharply, between what is obligatory and what is laudable but optional: in Catholicism, it had the unfortunate effect of offering a two-tier morality, one for religious and another for the rest of humankind; it wasn't of a piece.

The virtue approach knows its own limitations: it knows that the possession of practical wisdom or *phronesis* (which was the ancient term) cannot be taken for granted but must be won, and that this only comes through a continuing openness to goodness and faithful practice. That is part of the paradox: it is only the one who has learned how to be good who can be wise, who can know what goodness is. A virtue approach seems to me to be a necessary component of an adequate moral life, which I see as a matter of listening to our deepest self, of attention and imagination. But is it sufficient? We carry our meagre ration of goodness in earthen vessels. Perhaps we need to supplement it with more precise guidance. Perhaps we need prohibitions – frontiers – as well as encouragement in the path of virtue. I believe that rules, at least of a general kind, are intelligible and possible, and that they are important for society. Some rules, for example about the inviolability of the individual, will be a line in the sand for many people. It cannot but be a good attitude, also, to want to bring about the greatest amount of human good, if all the necessary safeguards are built in – but that is a major reservation. In fact, you will find that, in practice, there is coincidence between these two theories more often than the bare scaffolding of the theories might suggest. Perhaps it is a mistake to be a moral monist: different theories throw light on different situations.

So back, obliquely, to agape-love. It has been variously interpreted as overlapping exactly with one or other approach. One can see that it is easily regarded as an excellent virtue. Indeed there are some who see it as the central virtue of moral life and see other virtues as expressions of it. It has also been argued that it is in fact a form of consequences-morality: it requires the doing of the greatest good. Others combine it with rules (of natural law, for example). They see agape-love as the central rule and other rules as expressions or mediations of love. They argue that the Christian way is one of what they call 'in-principled love', or love expressed in rules. There are those, too, who claim that it coincides exactly with the celebrated principle that we treat others always as ends and never merely as means. Agape is compatible with different theories, but it seems to me that it needs them. And so Frankena's complaint, with which I opened this chapter, about the fuzziness of a love-ethic.

CHAPTER 11
The Thorny Matter of Absolutes

If I had a euro for the number of times I have been asked whether there are absolutes in morality, I'd be rich. Questions about absolute (or exceptionless) rules both bother and fascinate people. I can see why people ask: they come across situations in their own lives, or in the lives of others, that seem to justify not keeping a well-known moral rule, when, in fact, it seems cruel to insist on the rule.

We have noted that we can have general directions for our lives, such as: we should value truth, life, justice, fidelity, the sacredness of the person. You could imagine a society or teaching authority confining itself to such general, open-textured statements – they are a form of virtue ethics – and leaving people to work out the implications in their differing situations. So, for example, many people think that the Catholic Church should have confined itself to saying to married people that they should seek to live in a way that is fruitful for life and that is loving towards their spouse and their society (valuing life and love), without getting into detail like contraception. Of course, such broad directives do not solve knotty problems of living and do not tell us exactly what to do or avoid. So there will be genuine disagreement about what they commit us to. There is always debate, for example, about government budgets, levies and tax measures. The word that becomes the catch-cry on all sides is 'fairness'. An admirable thought, a moral concept: we should act fairly. But it is painfully obvious how difficult it is to agree on what it means. The devil is in the detail and we don't have detail in these general concepts.

Societies and churches have not been satisfied with general admonitions: they get into the detail, nailing down the general values in clear injunctions, especially of a negative kind – do not steal or kill or lie or divorce or commit adultery or engage in same sex relations. In the last chapter we called them rules. The Decalogue is the prime example. Such rule-statements simply describe a particular piece of behaviour and declare it to be wrong or right. It is quite clear what they mean. If I say it is immoral to kill anybody, or to utter what is contrary to what is in one's mind, or to have sexual relations with one who is not my spouse, there is no doubt what is in question. Whereas there is doubt if I say only that one should respect life, or truth, or be just or fair, or respect the meaning of human sexuality.

It is with these demanding rule-type statements that the greatest problems about absolutes arise. And they arise precisely because they are so determined. They really pin you down. There is no way of arguing about what such pieces of behaviour mean, as there is about what fairness or justice mean: the argument can only be about whether they are valid statements about morality or not, or whether there might be exceptions to them. Whether it is valid to say not only, 'do not kill' or 'it is wrong to divorce' as a generally valid piece of moral admonition, but to say 'do not ever kill or divorce'. The move from the general values to these very particular and especially absolute statements will be contested. But the Catholic Church does draw the line in certain crucial places. It has absolute rules about euthanasia, suicide, divorce, same-sex relations, direct sterilisation, direct abortion, embryonic stem cell research, sex outside marriage, lying, AIH, AID, and so on. It says that they are always wrong, in all possible circumstances. Or to use its language, they are 'intrinsically evil'. The question is: can such absolute rules be justified? Or might one find oneself in circumstances which would justify ignoring them?

Generally Valid or Absolute
Some will debate whether particular rules of this kind are valid at all. For example, they will question whether contraception is immoral of its very nature, as the Vatican says: they might say that it is morally indifferent,

so that the use of it is neither here nor there. Many will agree that some rules are acceptable as general statements of what is right or wrong, but not in an absolute fashion. That means that it is generally right to hold that one should not take another's property, or kill, or tell untruths, or divorce, but not always. You see, if you say that there are absolute or exceptionless rules, you are committing yourself to saying that circumstances could never arise in which a more important moral consideration would enter to complicate the situation. That is a big ask.

The problem is that life is complex and rules tend to oversimplify matters. As far back as Plato the question arose: if you have a sword that belongs to another but he is now mad, should you give it back to him? Obviously not. So the rule, 'give another what belongs to him' breaks down. And the reason it breaks down is that there is a feature of the situation, another moral consideration, to be attended to: which is, 'do not endanger human life'. Both cannot be observed together. Life is just like that. Likewise, there is debate both within and outside the churches about whether the rule, 'do not kill' breaks down in situations of war, self-defence and capital punishment. How many other traditional rules need to be modified? Many people, understandably, see absolute rules as a failure to appreciate the complexity of their lives. There are harrowingly difficult situations in which people have to act – we have plenty of stories, above all from situations of war, violence and upheaval, where people were faced with horrific choices – and increasingly in our own culture in situations of kidnapping and ransom demands, in intimidatory gang violence, in the drug culture. Not to mention more everyday examples.

So you might find yourself dissenting from some traditional rules. They may be too tightly stated, not acknowledging the complexity of life. They may be the result of baggage that a society has brought from the past. That has happened more in the area of sexuality, presumably because it was a key strand in church tradition. Some rules were influenced by cultural attitudes that are no longer acceptable, e.g. regarding the place and role of women or the understanding of marriage: note what we said about this in chapter four. However, to say that someone dissents from a rule does not mean that they do not seek the value that is meant to be promoted by the rule, only that the rule is too rigidly stated. Those who dissent from some traditional rules about sexuality may well appreciate its human significance, and value the handing on of life. They may be just as concerned about a trivialisation of sexuality and of the person as were *Humanae Vitae* and *Evangelium Vitae*. How to offer guidance is the problem. Values and ideals need to be preserved. But that may not be best addressed with absolute moral rules.

Let's tidy up some related points. (a) You might say: 'but isn't murder always immoral, isn't that an absolute?' Yes, that is valid and is an important general bulwark for society. But when examined, it is a tautologous statement. When is killing murder? Murder is unjust killing: but tell me precisely, when is killing unjust? Is it murder for a police officer to kill someone who has gone berserk with a gun and is randomly shooting in a supermarket? It is killing. But is it murder – unlawful, blameworthy? Does the officer lack respect for life, or is his act one that respects life? The same issue arises if one operates with a slippery, but often used, term like 'innocent' – it is immoral to kill the innocent. Of course. But we are left with the same issue: how do I define 'innocent'? Are combatants in war innocent, or is it morally legitimate to kill them, or the civilian population that manufactures the essentials of war, or a 'harmless' ('innocent') person who is about to kill or rape you, or a person who has committed heinous crimes of murder, or a 'terrorist' who is about to blow up half a city, or a foetus who is very likely to die and bring about the death of its mother? Which, if any, is innocent? So such statements about murder or innocence are not so clear after all.

(b) Other possible ways of trying to deal with the matter amount to the same thing. For example, do you say 'it is a lie to tell an untruth or speak a falsehood but lying can sometimes be justified'? Or do you say, 'I don't call telling an untruth a lie if the questioner has no right to the truth'. You have only redescribed the problem. In the first case, you give a neutral, material definition of lying – speaking a falsehood. In the second, you smuggle in difficult *moral* considerations about 'right to the truth' into your very definition of lying. When does another not have a right to the truth? How do you work that out?

(This is complicated stuff and I don't want to get bogged down. It is not a matter of balancing angels on the point of a needle or engaging in vacuous casuistry. What is important is to know what we and others mean by the terms we use. I think we have some experience of distinguishing killing and murder: we wait to see if someone who has killed is convicted of murder or is, for example, regarded as acting in self-defence. But in common parlance we use 'he stole' and 'he took what belongs to another' interchangeably. There are circumstances when one is entitled to take what belongs to another: some moralists would like to keep the term 'stealing' for situations in which one is not so justified. Then 'stealing is morally wrong' is tautologous, like murder, because in this view it is by definition unjust taking. Likewise, they would like to keep the term 'lying' for circumstances in which one utters an untruth without justification. Then 'lying is morally wrong' also becomes tautologous. It leaves you, of course, with the problem of spelling out exactly when taking or speaking falsehoods is unjustified. What is important is to define our terms.)[1]

1. Some authors argue that 'adultery is immoral' is analogous to a tautology, since, in Christian usage at least, the term 'adultery' means sexual relations by someone who is not morally free to have such relations except with the man or woman to whom they have vowed perpetual fidelity.

What If My Intention Is Good?

There is something else that complicates the matter, although it is only a different angle on what we have been discussing. When we try to make a moral assessment of something, we are talking most obviously about the action that is to be done – to tell the truth, to have sexual intercourse, to pay a debt, to take a life, to keep a confidence, to take someone's character. About the moral act. But suppose I want to do something that falls under the rule and on the face of it looks immoral, but I do it for what might be regarded as a laudable motive, or in a set of circumstances that changes the overall shape of the act. I break a confidence knowing and intending that it will prevent great harm. I tell an untruth to deceive the enemy. I torture a terrorist to elicit information that is crucial to the safety of millions. I have contraceptive intercourse to save my marriage. I use a condom to avoid infecting my partner with the Aids virus. I allow a disabled new born child to die in order to save it much suffering. It is a common enough form of argument, but rules-talk tends not to take kindly to it, whereas it is more congenial to the greatest-good approach, and has all the dangers associated with that. Does my intention justify my action? Will it do to plead that I meant well?

Some say that it is simply wrong to break a confidence, to tell an untruth, to torture, to have extra-marital intercourse, to use contraception, to kill or allow another to die, and they don't want to hear anything about circumstances or intentions: they take a narrow view of the moral act. There are others who say that it is only when you have taken account of the whole complexity of what is involved that you can make a moral judgment. That means that nothing is decided until everything is decided. You cannot be satisfied with the bare description of the brute fact or act – this is killing, this is telling an untruth, this is breaking a confidence, this is contraceptive intercourse. You need a human description, which would include the intention: so, according to this view, you cannot say that any of these acts is wrong until you make a wider assessment. They see the intention as possibly bringing in an issue of moral significance. So the question of what we mean by the-moral-act-that-is-to-be-assessed becomes more difficult. You have to weigh the conflicting elements of the situation, and the intention may be one of them: this can be an agonising decision; it has nothing to do with soft options.

Some theologians regard this kind of assessment as a valid form of moral argument, but it is a matter of great debate. It would be naïve to suggest that there are easy answers and I am giving a greatly simplified account of the matter. There are those, as will have appeared in the previous chapter, who regard the approach as entirely unjustified. The Vatican, in the encyclical *Veritatis Splendor*, in an effort to protect its teaching about the intrinsic evil of some acts, has intervened to adjudicate, and has also condemned it: it insists on a narrower account of the moral act.[2] Its fear, I imagine, is that such thinking reduces everything in morals to the intention and, if facilely employed, justifies anything and everything. That is an understandable fear – good intentions alone, or good outcomes alone, are not a sufficient justification in morals. But it is not decisive and key debates about moral theory will continue. It needs to be said, also, that some prominent Catholic theologians were unhappy about the account of the views attributed to them in that encyclical.[3]

So Can You Have Rules?

All that might seem to lead to hopelessness, as if there were no clear answers. There are. We should remember that moralists are often concerned about limit situations, where exceptional circumstances raise a question about a rule. They are testing the rule in hypothetical situations and covering all imaginable possibilities. Many of the rules which our traditions, Christian and societal, have handed down – about killing, theft, truth, life, sexuality – are to be trusted. They have the presumption of validity: they are the wisdom of the ages. For the bulk of our lives, they will see us through. You could call them practical absolutes. It is worth noting, however, that if questions are raised about the absolute validity of such

2. *Veritatis Splendor* 79.
3. See, for example, the series of articles in *The Tablet*, Oct–Dec 1993.

rules, this is not from a desire to be soft on morality, or careless, or 'liberal', or to go along with the crowd. It is a matter of acknowledging the complexity of life. It is about being moral, deciding what to do when you are faced with what seem to be opposing moral demands, when, for example, it is impossible both to protect life and truth (as when the Gestapo come around), when you are trying to work out what is the more serious moral demand. All moral demands are serious, but they are not all of the same gravity. It is a matter of the weight to be given to different values and the rules which enshrine them.

When this kind of debate arises, people sometimes say, 'well, isn't it alright if the person involves thinks it is alright?' That is a different question and obscures the issue. I'll come to it in the chapter on conscience. The point here is that there is an alrightness of an action before or independently of what the person involved thinks. It is what the ideal observer, some perfect, all-wise judge of the matter would say – the objective morality of the situation. That is what we are after at the moment. Just how wc, far from perfect and far from wise, can make the best shot at it is what we are discussing here.

CHAPTER 12
The Emphases of Our Morality: What Matters Most?

Enough of absolutes. Questions about them are inescapable. But there has been undue concentration on them, especially in church circles. That tends to limit our vision to particular subjects and critical situations. Moral life, as we have seen, is a much richer, a much more demanding, a much more dynamic enterprise. Something that might be worth considering is this. If we look at our rules, or virtues, or notion of the common good – our moral tradition – what do we see as important, what in our outlook on morality carries the greatest weight, and, conversely, what draws the greatest reproach or sanction? How do our different moral prescriptions rate? It is our rules, and especially our absolutes, that create the institutional climate in which we live. They have an educative influence – for good or ill. They give us our sense of who the good person is. How wise were they?

It is now rather trite to say that the landscape of our lives has changed. Very obviously, religious adherence which so buttressed our notion of moral obligation has diminished. More subtly, we do not have the same sense that there is an order of things, in some way associated with God – a mythic road-map, a tribal vision, that situates the person in a larger context and colours what is seen as the worthwhile life. There is something in the air today that says that we ourselves can determine and establish what life will be about: popular culture and psychology seem to tell us to do our own thing, to seek our own individual way, our own self-realisation. There is a celebration of freedom, a willingness to live with uncertainty, an itch to experiment, an impatience with being in the same job in the same place, an urge to explore different ways and cultures. Much of it dictated by the comprehensive globalisation of our lives. There has been a weakening of structures that upheld us – neighbourhood, family, religion, culture. And a loss of esteem for, a feeling of betrayal by, traditional sources of guidance – church, state, banks, politicians, invest-ment managers, advisers of different kinds.

Some of that is good, some bad, but all of it influential in the moral sphere. We are far from the staid, ordered, unquestioning climate which took traditional forms of morality for granted. A social climate that values self-authorisation and choice translates into a search for more personally committed forms of devotion and practice: to be self-authenticating, rather than submissive, is considered to be a condition of true humanness.

There are problems here but there are valuable concerns also. Problems, if we settle for a narrow self-realisation as the goal of human life and fail to recognise where authenticity in living lies. There is a rough structure to human nature and to human flourishing which cannot be ignored. That is where we find our bearings: the right way of valuing human living is not simply up to us. The greatest danger is that we would sell ourselves short, settle for an attenuated concept of the person, let the spiritual slip out of the very definition of our identity as humans, i.e. ignore what is most characteristically human and significant. It is important that we have a framework to our lives in which some things matter more, are higher or deeper, more worthy of admiration than others, and that therefore we are not immediately open to every wind of desire and allurement that blows. It is what we count important that defines our identity, who we are in ourselves. It is only if we acknowledge the attractiveness of the good, the inviolability of others, the duties of citizenship, the interdependence of all humankind, the needs of the less fortunate, the cosmic order, that we will find an identity that is not trivial.

But there are valuable concerns in our culture also. You find a search – often in odd and oblique ways – for the deep things, for meaning, for something worth living for, for the richness of being human. You hear a desire for wholeness, integration, spirituality, synthesis in life, a need for some overarching vector, to 'get it all together'. There are new concerns. If our youth quietly ignore what they see as the frumpish morality of their elders, if they have found a comfortable place for divorce, pre-marital and same-sex relationships, they are more sensitive to other aspects of relationships and other virtues. It seems that what commands respect now are the qualities of justice, fairness, tolerance, an acknowledgement of freedom and rights, an appreciation of nature, an anger at hypocrisy and narrowness. There is an expansion of moral considerations – and a relativising. The old ways do not resonate.

> I assert the right of love to choose,
> from whatever race, or place. And of verse
> to allay, to heal, our tribal curse, that narrowness.[1]

I am not contending that what people say or think is an infallible guide to morality. Nor am I saying that freedom is the only value or some kind of absolute: we have to reason together about the meaning of the good life, about the right way to value things. What I am talking about rather is the lived Christian experience of faithful people, and their right to re-evaluate traditional positions. That involves a redefining of who we are, of what is most important for society, about the common good. It will make, at least, for a change of emphasis.

1. John Montague, 'Last Court'.

There is a different list of the seven deadly sins in a world which will recognise, for example, that a same sex or pre-marital relationship that is characterised by justice, equality and fidelity may well be a more moral way than a traditional morality that lacks such qualities. This is not to say that a new morality will simply jettison all traditional concerns. It cannot. Because some of the traditional norms clearly enshrine what respect for the other must mean. And it is interesting that if people are asked to elaborate a morality for the future they will often come up with something akin to the old forms. But new thinking will broaden the traditional, will humanise it, and will have modifications to make.

An undertow to all this, I think, is a frustration at the failure in our moral *milieu* to have a righteous indignation at dishonesty and exploitation in their various guises. A chasm has appeared in modern life between the claim that something is legal, and therefore legitimate (financial dealings, banking guidelines and practices, government departmental regulations etc.), and a concern for morality. People wonder how this could happen. It points up the inadequacy of traditional notions and says much about the history of our moral education. There is disillusionment now, and one hopes that it is disillusionment with rampant liberalism. I have heard more mention of the common good in recent months than for a long time. The realisation is slowly growing that what matters in morality, and what moral guides should concern themselves with are the virtues that are crucial to a just, honest and flourishing society. We need that: there are deeply embedded inequalities in our society which are corrosive of civic virtue. There is a task for education here and for those who believe that they have a moral mission.

Morality cannot be a list of precepts. But it was easier to talk morality, and especially to talk sin, in relation to such. Here is something worth pondering. The Catholic Church is often accused of preaching only about sexual sin and neglecting other areas, such as justice – and there is no doubt that for long ages its attitude to sexuality was both negative and intrusive. What is interesting, however, is that the accusation flies in the face of recent history: there have been many more Vatican statements in the last half-century or more about justice, rights and the environment than about sexuality – and when did you last hear a sermon on sexuality? And yet, something is awry. The problem has been that teaching on sexuality has been unambiguous about specific, well-defined, acts, while that on justice has been well-intentioned, but largely aspirational. And, dare I say, not seen to be a priority in church practice. Orthopraxis, as they say, is as significant as orthodoxy: what we do as a church is as important as what we teach; it is a condition of credibility. One consequence has been that the notion of a Catholic ethos, despite the richness of the Christian vision, has been confined largely to sexual sin, when it ought to be just as certainly about justice, tolerance and understanding.

This is one of the reasons why a virtue approach to morality is appealing. It offers a coherent, richer, more integrated view of living. It makes room for the great Christian stories which enrich our moral imagination. It allows us to see that whatever particular rules we find necessary for the common good grow organically out of values that are native to us, and are not some kind of diktat. It catches better than, say, a rules approach, the attitudes we have been looking at and that seem to belong to a comprehensive moral life – honesty, integrity, humility before creation etc. These are necessary if we are to chart a new way for morality and for a realignment in the weight we give to different moral attitudes. It is when we set out from listening to the call of our deepest selves – and for some that will mean a self enlarged by the Christian vision – about what it means to be a person in society with a care for the common good, rather than settling for a restricted hand-me-down morality, that such a range of moral life reveals itself. It puts what I have said about absolutes in context. One cannot deny that they are important, controversial, and that they affect some lives acutely. But they are about the frontier of death rather than about beauty of life.

CHAPTER 13
Moral Agent: Who Am I? How Free Am I?

What we have been doing up to now is trying to plot the way of moral living. That involved looking at the ideals that are called for by our life in society – the great virtues encouraged by both religious and non-religious traditions. But it also required something about the kind of decision-making that is involved in the complex decisions of everyday life. All that has been about what is theoretically right or wrong, to be admired and aspired towards, or to be done or avoided. I have already called that objective morality. But however much we may need to lay out this theoretical level, we need also to engage with how in fact people like ourselves make moral decisions – and, to push this a bit further – how in doing so they become moral persons and develop character, and how that character affects their interpretation of their moral situation. That is what I hope to do in this chapter. Human beings are not machines, but living, breathing, thinking animals with their own strikingly particular story. That is the lens through which they see the moral landscape. So I want to consider what a person will see of the moral demand, or more precisely, will be able to see. I say 'able to see' designedly. We may not have the freedom that is necessary in order to see truthfully. Seeing is not just a matter of intelligence, of having the capacity to make a sharp analysis of the factors of a situation. Emotions enter in: those who are normally regarded as intelligent people are often emotionally pathetic and not very wise.

Moral judgment is a particular kind of judgment. It is a judgment of what I must do (the moralists call it a judgment of practical intellect). It engages me in a way that speculative judgment does not. If you ask me what I think about the poetry of Seamus Heaney or the art of Rothko or the relative merits of Ronaldo and Kaka, I can probably give my opinion without feeling that it commits me to anything. But to see and make a moral judgment – that I should leave this exciting relationship, or forgive my abuser, or admit to my sneaky dishonesty, or acknowledge my jealousy, or bury the hatchet, or return my bank bonus, or share with the less well-off – that is a different kind of matter altogether. Confronting a moral decision is not only a rational but an affective process. It engages me in a way that speculative judgment does not. It is the kind of thing that, depending on the circumstances, threatens me, frightens me, hurts me, diminishes me, exposes me to ridicule, loses me esteem, weakens my security – and so on. Very likely, I don't want to go there. And that may well prevent me even from seeing what I must do.

Story
It depends on who I am. I am not talking about my name or about the fact that I am an individual agent in the world. I am talking about who I have become with my unique configuration of desires, fears, prejudices, longings, hurts, jealousies, envies. It is not a clean slate that takes on the burden of moral life. But a very particular person, heavy with the legacy of its past – the person I considered in chapter three. We only see this if we see life as a process. We have tended to think of ourselves as doers of a considerable number of discrete acts, good or bad, for which we will be judged. Our moral life is more subtle and complex. It is not a matter of acts that we can leave behind us, as if they did not leave their mark on us. They embed themselves. Through them we make ourselves. Through the moments and minutes of our thoughts and actions we weave that tapestry, and it is difficult to unweave what we have done. The desires, fears and values of our personality are not eccentric or without an explanation: they are the history of our lives – think, for example, how early sexual experiences shape sexual identity and desire. We may not be very responsible for what we have made – things happen to us. But, one way or the other, consciously or unconsciously,

thinkingly or unthinkingly, we have become someone.
We see, judge, respond, in line with that. So that at any
stage of my journey I can see what I can see and do what
I can do.

Why do emotions unhinge us so much – for good or
ill? Notice that they are *about* something – we are angry
at or excited *by*. They ascribe great importance to something. Their arousal is explained by my life's project, by
what I deeply feel is crucial for my well-being and
happiness, even if others consider it bizarre. So we are
different characters. For example, it may be mightily
important for one of us to be known as virtuous, or
knowledgeable, or to feel esteemed, or best loved, or
special, or nice, or a tough man, or a cool dude. It reveals
the concerns of my heart. How I came to be like this is
lost in the twilight of my past, but these are now my
evaluative beliefs. If you touch me in what is *my*
particularly sensitive area, if you shatter this world of
mine, I suffer an emotional upheaval, a kind of
annihilation. What the upheaval tells is that there is a
lot at stake here. The effect of this is that we cannot see.
We cannot make clean judgments about our situations.
We might be able to make them about other people's
situation – usually, there is nothing at stake for us there!
The central point of this chapter is to say that feelings
or emotional hunger affect moral life. They will support
moral insight or they will distort reason at successive
stages – in marshalling and censoring facts, in

understanding situations, in deciding what is to be done – the steps in which the moralist is crucially interested.

So we are not cool choosers. But let's not be entirely negative about emotions: they are a gift to our moral selves. Truth exercises its own attraction. Goodness has its own emotional pull. It is surely a gift that we are bodily and deeply aroused by injustice or cruelty or beauty or love. Not to experience this, not to be inclined by emotion, is to be morally impaired. Feelings of empathy engender understanding. Feelings of anger awaken us to injustice and the need for action. In the morally converted, feelings are sensitive to values. In the virtuous, moral behaviour is accompanied by feelings of joy and satisfaction. So that it is important that we be exposed to beauty, generosity and nobility, not only in art and nature but in people. Our imagination seduces us to goodness, as well as to evil, even magically in the imaginative life of the theatre or cinema or story. Our affections can be educated. It was not rules or duty that inspired the Good Samaritan: he was moved to pity (moved in his bowels, as the Greek puts it) and he acted creatively.

Too often, it is the other way, the way of distortion. Our better moments, our judgments, are in constant danger of being swamped by the fears and desires which dispute with us the control of our lives – how will I manage if I am unpopular or insecure or unnoticed? These old patterns or ways of being constantly emerge to bully us. They come uninvited.

... how difficult it is to remain just one person
for our house is open, there are no keys in the
doors,
and invisible guests come in and out at will.[1]

We cannot make space for ourselves. It is easier, safer,
not to risk breaking free to the different life which might
be beckoning. So that, like St Paul, we frustratingly find
ourselves doing the things we don't want to do, unable
to do what we want to do. It is in some part the story of
every life. It was too easily assumed in the past, I
think, that everybody could see the cogency of moral
argument. So that failure to accept it, or respond to it,
was regarded as a matter of stupidity or bad faith. That
failed to recognise not only the subtlety of moral
argument but, much more so, the actuality of the one
who judges.

We are not isolated free choosers, monarchs of all we
survey, but benighted creatures sunk in a reality
whose nature we are constantly and overwhelmingly
tempted to deform by fantasy ... Our current picture
of freedom encourages a dream-like facility; whereas
what we require is a renewed sense of the difficulty
and complexity of the moral life and the opacity of
persons ... Simone Weil said that morality was a

1. Czesław Miłosz, 'Ars Poetica?'

matter of attention not of will. We need a new vocabulary of attention.[2]

Freedom To See: Freedom To Do

What we are talking about here is a form of freedom. We usually think in terms of our freedom to act, to do something. But behind and before that there is what might be called our freedom to see and judge. They are closely intertwined and perhaps it is unrealistic to separate them but let us distinguish for a moment. Seeing – wanting to see – is the first great difficulty in morals. We are only half-free or half-willing seekers of truth: the factors which inhibit our freedom of action inhibit first our freedom to see. We have great difficulty in seeing things as they are and not as we would like them to be. Objectivity is not natural to us. We say about people that they are – at times or even as a general pattern – angry, anxious, optimistic, dependent, cautious, scrupulous, hurt, excitable, spontaneous, easily frightened. We imply that they will tend to see something harmful or frightening or threatening or exciting in a situation where others might not see it. That will affect how they read situations.

Even when we do in some fashion see the way of truth, we have to ask ourselves how free we are to do it. There are extreme notions that say that we are not free

2. Murdoch, 'Against Dryness', in Peter Conradi (ed.), *Existentialists and Mystics*, New York, 1999, 287–96 .

at all. Certainly, we may be less free than we think. But generally we acknowledge a basic freedom: we distinguish acts that we perform with intention from those performed inadvertently.[3] Society has gradually expanded notions of unfreedom to include not only the well-know external pressures but many internal pressures – the buried patterns of our emotional lives. They are often the clue to why we acted and even – as we shall see – to what kind of act we performed from a moral, and at times, from a legal point of view. So much so that when we know something of the emotional life of another we can almost predict how they will act. How often have I heard people say that such and such a one would not make a good government minister, or chief executive, or school principal, or hospital matron, or superior, or football manager, because he/she would buckle under stress, or couldn't escape self-aggrandisement, or couldn't take conflict, or couldn't face the untidy emotion of having to confront another, or couldn't make decisions for fear of making the wrong one. They might know what is the right thing to do, but they are shackled by their emotions. Unfree. We are all somewhere on a continuum of freedom-unfreedom.

People ask about freedom mostly in the context of praise and blame. That is important, but freedom has

3. 'The ways of thinking by which we thus distinguish between what can and what cannot be helped, and the opinions we build on them about actions and agents, may be rough and fallible, but they are absolutely essential for human life.' Midgley, op. cit., 56.

THE CALL TO BE HUMAN

wider implications. Morality is not just about performing acts. There is a vast spectrum of more or less morally valuable acts. It is possible to get people to go through or refrain from certain actions that look like cases of acting morally, either by inducing fear – what has been called *la pastorale de peur* – or by pandering to some morally irrelevant desire. But the value of this is doubtful: after all, you could get your dog to bring a loaf or a bottle of brandy to alleviate someone's distress. The background to such considerations is something that I gestured to in preceding chapters. It is the distinction between the right and the good: between just doing the right thing (which could be done for a variety of motives) and doing it out of goodness or virtue; a morality couched in terms of precept/law emphasises right, as does a morality closely related to discipline/ punishment. Goodness is a different matter.

It must be an ideal for us to make our lives authentic and autonomous, to arrive at the point where choices and acts are genuinely our own, a free response to true values. When we ask, from a moral point of view, *what* a person did, it may be just as important to ask *why*. Our feelings can 'get us' to perform what look like good acts when, in fact, they spring not from a genuine response to values but from the urgings of some less admirable emotions. We know how human respect, the emotional inability to say 'no', the fear of being thought a fool, the fear of what others will say, not to mention the influence of more obvious – even religious – fears can get us to perform acts that have only the shell of goodness. People in the caring professions are aware that their caring may be more a response to their own emotional needs than a genuine concern for others. The more disturbing fact is the unconscious stuff, a whole tissue of motives, the residue of childhood anxieties and fears that are the real springs of our actions, that are hidden from us, and that militate against mature morality. Certainly, any day we manage to prevent someone from murdering or maiming another, or any day we ourselves are persuaded, is a good day, however we are persuaded: fear, threat, restraint are sometimes necessary. Which is why we have moral rules in our societies. But the ideal is something more than, more interior than, that. Most of us will never fully reach its purity: our moral lives will remain an odd mix, but it is no harm to keep it ahead of us. If we are interested in the quality of our lives, interested in *goodness*, we have to be concerned about motive.

Enlightenment

So freedom to see, freedom to do. It is a way of looking at the project of our lives. The great traditions speak of it as a project of enlightenment, as deliverance from illusion about the kind of life that is worthwhile. Enlightenment is not a speculative matter. It includes a willingness, because we don't see unless we are willing – not hedging our bets, not keeping aces up our sleeve. But open to truth, whatever it be for us. This is perhaps what is most difficult, *to want to know*, to want the truth for my life, to be willing to allow myself to be chosen by the good, whatever it costs. What we must hope for is some transformation of ourselves, the development of habits of thought and feeling, which will conspire to enable us to be caring and courageous agents in our societies.

The sages tell us to trust our deep, or higher, or true self. There is nothing esoteric about this. I take it to mean listening to our wholeness, to all of who we are. The person I normally take myself to be – that busy, anxious little self, so preoccupied with its goals, fears and desires – is not even remotely the whole of who I am, and to seek the fulfilment of my life at this level is to miss out on the larger life. It is a matter of growing in a different level of consciousness. I mean a consciousness or sense of self that is a different way of seeing and valuing, a different set of preferences, one that is not absorbed by or slave to our more acquisitive and competitive energies. That promises us a fuller, more satisfactory life. Again, there is nothing esoteric about this: I write in the depths of a recession, in which commentators of all hues are advising us to do a bit of re-evaluating and think a bit more deeply about what we need and why – *seeing* differently, I suppose. That is only a hope for most of us. But we can't afford not to aspire to it. It is a consciousness that is waiting to be awakened in us. To try to engage it in some tentative, fragmented fashion is for us the moral call.

It has to be admitted that the factors that conspire against us are not just narrowly personal. It is not

possible to understand the psychic wounds which
inhibit the response of mind and heart without taking
account of the social and economic conditions in which
it has to be made: the individual person cannot be fully
healed apart from society's healing and wholeness; one
cannot leap out of one's situation and gaze on the
resplendent moral law. Human growth and morality
cannot be divorced from politics. So, programmes that
try to transform consciousness, that create justice, that
encourage self-esteem, that lift depression, that kindle
hope, are allies of morality. The whole *Zeitgeist* of
capitalist modernity, too, with its characteristic liberal
individual ethos, subtly undermines us. Not that I would
want to decry something like the Celtic Tiger. It did
enhance the lives of many, if not all equally. The danger
is a slide into a loss of soul and an accentuation of greed,
envy and competitiveness. A weakening of a sense of
human community. We might forget who we are. We
are all in constant need of decentring ourselves, of
recognising our true place in the cosmos.

> Kevin feels the warm eggs, the small breast, the
>   tucked
> Neat head and claws and, finding himself linked
> Into the network of eternal life
> Is moved to pity.[4]

4. Heaney, 'St Kevin and the Blackbird'.

THE CALL TO BE HUMAN

Transformation

How we might personally move towards greater freedom – educate our desires – has been a puzzle down the ages. There are things that help. Example, training, story, hagiography, prayer (provided it is not the babbling of words) are important, and perhaps, especially, our inspiring biblical stories: we saw earlier how sensitive they are to the very frailties which we have been discussing here. It is a matter of entering into, and trying to share, their spirit. We have age-old ways of doing that, some of them newly burnished today in such practices as *lectio divina*. The stories are given force by the conviction that others have lived them more completely than us – that it is possible, that there is hope. That, I think, is part of what it means to belong to a church or tradition. Different world-views read the human condition differently. Some are nihilistic, some pessimistic. Christianity is realistic but hopeful, inspirational but patient: it believes in the enlivening presence of God within us. The great Christian story is that God loves each of us as other, unconditionally. It says that we live in a universe in which every human being is supremely important and, in the most fundamental manner, equal. The hope is that if we could feel this in the marrow bone it would have a healing effect, a deepening of our sense of self. And that it would enable a new attitude to one another, an engagement with the other that is non-combative and noncompetitive, that does not need to win or possess. At least, it offers us hope in our night.[5]

The traditions are unyielding in their insistence on meditative life – attention, presence, awareness – which allows us to be intimate witnesses of our own foolishness, and to collude with our good angels.

> Moral change comes from an *attention* to the world whose natural result is a decrease in egoism through an increased sense of the reality of, primarily of course other people, but also other things ... Change of being, metanoia, is not brought about by straining and 'will-power', but by a long deep process of unselfing.[6]

Meditative states of deep wonder, sorrow or beauty open our hearts: in those moments we are more aware of the

5. '[God] loves to perfection without a fault, without an error, from beginning to end ... In the end I not only discover that another was loving me before I loved, and thus that this other already played the lover before me, but above all I discover that this first lover, from the very beginning, is named God.' Marion, op. cit., 222.
'The Jewish and Christian traditions ... speak of a personal agency without need or desire shaping finite and temporal agents, agents at whose centre is "the image of God", the capacity for reflecting God's gratuitous making-possible of the life of what is other ... a God who can't be negotiated with, who has no interest to defend and whose creative activity is therefore pure gratuity.' Rowan Williams, *Lost Icons: Reflections on Cultural Bereavement*, London, 2003, 197–8.
6. Murdoch, 'Fact and Value', *Metaphysics*, 52ff. (italics original).

unity of all being and of the kind of persons we are meant to be. They let compassion and empathy grow and soften our hearts. To seek this path is an act of faith in our possibilities. This does not mean escaping from our inner conflicts to higher, more lofty, more 'spiritual' thoughts. They'll come if we engage with our own chaos. Freud would have us, as Auden puts it, 'remember most of all to be enthusiastic over the night ... because it needs our love' – our own night, of course.[7] Or as Rowan Williams puts it, 'If we don't know how to attend to the reality that is our own inner turmoil, we shall fail in responding to the needs of someone else.'[8] It is a common mistake of people of religion – but not only of such – to confuse the levels of their lives. Dealing with the emotional life is often messy, painful and protracted, so that many spiritual ways try to bypass it and jump directly to the so-called spiritual realm. It is a mistake about the geography of our human agency, about how the tangled undergrowth of our old patterns ensnares us. We are body-spirit, not split, not dualist. We cannot escape the everyday turmoil. We need to deal with the knots that prevent a serene relationship with others and with our God.

The age-old wisdom is that awareness will patiently resolve things – the therapist, the moral teacher and the spiritual tradition agree on that. But only, I think, if it is a deep and suffering awareness, as we track back the story

7. W.H. Auden, 'In Memory of Sigmund Freud'.
8. Rowan Williams, *Silence and Honey Cakes*, Oxford, 2003, 26.

of our lives and come to know in a new way the fears and hurts which inhabit us. It is a long road and there is no guarantee of success. It will need a forgiveness of ourselves, an acceptance of our own tortuous story and of the particular torque of our own lives. Life won't change much and neither shall we. We shall not suddenly arrive to broad, sunlit uplands. It will not do to wallow in self-pity: our salvation is in engaging the 'now' of our lives, in hearing the moral call in the present. We all have promises to keep. But awareness is already a freeing from the prison of our blindness. It gives us psychic space. It can open a way.

Lectures or talk or books won't do it: indeed they may only distract us into mistaking information for transformation. It is easy to talk the talk. There is a difference between learning about virtue and practising it: the former can be a delusive substitute for the real thing. I suspect that, for the generality, the constricting demons are not cast out either by prayer and fasting alone. You meet people who tell you that they pray a lot, frequent the sacraments, perform pious practices, but who wonder despairingly why they are still so difficult, so unloving, so much of a headache to themselves and to others. I am sure there are miracles, but we cannot count on them or demand them: we have to be open to the conditions of our humanity, to take the human means of moral growth. As the quotation from Murdoch above suggests, it is not a matter of straining and 'will-power'. By indirections we might find directions out. The range of more subtle approaches is the grace of God abroad in the world.

CHAPTER 14
Conscience and Choice

Every now and again the issue of conscience bubbles up in our newspapers and gives rise to sharp debate. There are good historical reasons why we should make a fuss about it and I'll come to that later. Let us note, first, the wide variety of ways we talk about conscience – 'consulting conscience', 'informing conscience', 'freedom of conscience', 'the voice of conscience', 'conscience the voice of God', 'the rights of conscience', 'following conscience', 'conscientious objection'. What is confusing is that conscience is made to look like a special faculty or piece of equipment which we possess. If that is the image we have, then the most useful thing we could say about conscience is that there is no such thing. We are conscious of many things in life: my conscience is my consciousness or awareness of the moral demand in me. We are referring to the manner in which this is grasped or appropriated by each of us, to my realisation that I must do the good, that it is impossible to go on being a human being and bury that. It is not so much that I have a conscience as that I am a conscience. That is how I experience myself as a human being. That is an inescapable fact of my life.[1]

The Quality of Conscience

I am a conscience. So are you. We are talking about the same inescapable human thrust. But my awareness is mine. It is different from yours or anybody else's. The conscience of each of us has its own special quality and range. We might explore the matter by looking at these two aspects. First then, the quality of our conscience. It helps to think about conscience in terms of age or history. We talk about the moral sense of children. It is important that they be trained, that a moral way be proposed to them, that they learn notions of right or good. But one may wonder what morality means to them, about the quality of their morality. Morality for a child may be a matter of doing what they are told, of pleasing parents, of reward and punishment, of approval and disapproval. That is all they are capable of. You could only call it morality in a very limited sense. As they grow older, a different awareness of living comes to them. They have to reckon with society and its

---

1. *'Conscience is not a colonial governor imposing alien norms*; it is our nature itself, become aware of its own underlying pattern.' Midgley, *Beast and Man: The Roots of Human Nature*, London, 1979, 274 (italics original).

traditions and norms: the societal values of justice, order, equality and fairness challenge them. To respond to that is a lot. But there is a further stage beyond that, where, if they are lucky, they grow in autonomy, internalise values, become more self-directive. It is a more human, more personal style of conscience.

The conscience of an adult may remain at any one of these stages. We may go through our lives as passive, compliant figures. What is perhaps most frustrating is the manner in which old authority directives from childhood cling to us – what some call the super-ego. The little boy or little girl whose life was bounded by parental love or disapproval, whose happiness or unhappiness revolved around that, amazingly still has echoes of this in the adult psyche. The authority figures have long gone. But the echoes are still there, long ago interiorised, now one's own. They come with the same sense, the same fear, and the same guilt as genuine conscience. They cling to us. It is humiliating. Even when we are aware and try to beat them off, they mock us with their clinginess. So that our psyche is in constant need of spring-cleaning.

We are all somewhere in the continuum. To some extent our particular kind of conscience is made for us because we absorb so much of the point of view, values and prejudices of our culture and background. We may have been lucky or unlucky. To some other extent we make our own conscience as we act on the 'givens' of life. How we arrived at it is our own slow and fitful journey. I am not referring mainly to the correctness of our judgments, the kind of code we have, but to the whole inner sense of moral responsibility, to the manner in which we create our moral life. This brings together many issues which we have seen – our personal notion of morality, our world-view, our story, our moral theory, our virtue, the nature of our moral acts, our motivation – in general *why* and *how* we do what we do. I take it that we don't want to remain with a childish conscience, that we might even hope to get beyond a social conscience. And I take it that we would like to sweep annoying super-ego fears out of our lives.

What we are looking for is authentic response to the experience of life. Genuine morality can only be that which arises out of personal maturity and responsibility: that is the conscience of one who has taken on the burden of existence, who is open to moral conside-rations, who wrestles with the ambiguity of life. That is a very tall order. But I take it that in some fashion this is what it means to be a person, what a characteristically human life looks like. This more humanly evolved life is the thrust of the God-given evolutionary process. Most of us are a long way off. At best our response is a mixed matter. We do not have that aliveness to authentic living. Many of us just drift. We do not want to know what is good for us and for others. We are too wounded, too needy, too fearful, too wary, too uncentred. Goodness wants to express itself in us but we are afraid of where it will lead us. Our natural taste for the truth is smothered by our fantasies.

Much discussion on conscience short-circuits that basic responsibility. It may easily give the impression that if you think something is alright, then it is alright. That has a truth but it does not do full justice to the human endeavour. The drama of our lives is about what kind of people we have become. It is in the mysterious hinterland of our psyche that the real responsibility lies. That is the obligation within obligation, the duty within duty – to open ourselves to the higher forces, however (religiously or not) we conceive them. Often our failures are not so much in the discrete moments of decision, but long before that in the readiness or lack of it. Which is why, 'if you think it is OK, it is OK' is wide of the mark. It is what lies before and in between the acts that is crucial: we have a responsibility around that. Only the morally converted are ready to let the truth into their hearts. And certainly only the morally converted are ready to do it. Which brings us back to that tantalising question of earlier chapters: why cannot we be moral; how can we become moral?

Some of the discussion about conscience fits more easily into a morality of precept and permission. It looks like, 'am I allowed to do this?', 'will I be reproached if I do it?', 'is it a sin?' Somewhere in the background is the notion of someone who controls morality – perhaps God or a church. In our religious tradition there is often a search for an obliging priest, or confessor. Fine, if you think of it as talking to a spiritual guide – who like all best guides will mirror back your life to you, who will facilitate an attitude of seriousness, who will encourage responsibility. That can be important: it sometimes enables people to cast off a burden of guilt that they should never have had in the first place. But conscience judgment cannot be about permissions or soft options. It is more like the opening out of vistas. It is about who we want to be in the world, about our possibilities and responsibilities for society, for the cosmos, for the future. And for the Christian, it is about allowing the great broad call of our God-stories, and the inspiration of those who lived them, to influence us. It is about the fruits of the Spirit, about the love poured into our hearts. Making ethical judgments, for example, will not always be about who is right and who is wrong, who has the rights and who the responsibilities. There are ways – imaginative ways of reconciliation and mediation and compromise and gratuitousness. Nobody can free you from your responsibility, can take on the burden of your conscience. It is a lonely call.

Is conscience then the voice of God, as we are often told? Well, yes, if you think of your whole moral life as the inescapable project of being flung into existence with, as Aquinas strikingly puts it, a share in the divine reason, an inner law of conscience to guide and challenge. Yes, too, if you take the view that our moral lives are religious, that it is the place where we live our response to the Creator-God, whose cosmos we share with others. Yes, if we realise that God's love for each of his creatures makes a demand on our love. Yes, if we accept that we have a call to bring to completion the covenant of God for the humanisation of the world. No, if we think that the call of God arrows directly into our minds, without the grind of heart-searching for what is best. No, if we think that the voice of God is identical with the voice of authority or with some set of rules which we have to observe or enforce.

The Content of Conscience

So much for the quality of our conscience. What about the content of it, roughly the kind of moral code which we hold? Your conscience differs from mine. Perhaps we both recognise the broad range of virtues. But after that, there is bound to be disagreement. Quite apart from the personal scars that cloud our vision, morality is a difficult matter for anyone. There is plenty of room for legitimate difference. If we recall some general issues from earlier chapters – we may genuinely disagree about moral theory, about the range of morality, about what facts are relevant to a situation, about the weight to be given to different values, about what cases are exceptional. And any of us can think up dozens of particular issues in our personal and societal lives which do not admit of clear or easy answers. With the best will in the world we will disagree with one another, and with authorities. And we may well get it wrong. It is a pity if we do. It creates problems for ourselves, for our society, for the future. But that's life.

Some have developed a lax conscience that is morally obtuse. Some have a scrupulous conscience that fearfully sees responsibilities where there are none, or worries pointlessly about the past. Others have grown into a genuinely sensitive conscience, its antennae delicately attuned to the widest range of moral considerations. Most of us, I suspect, are rather patchy – assiduous in some areas of morality, blind in others. We compartmentalise our lives rather easily. There can even be a frightening schizophrenia, and what is even more frightening is that one can somehow rationalise evil conduct. We hear of people who are generous and self-sacrificing in one sphere of their lives, cruel and destructive in another.

On a more general level, one wonders about traditions that seem to limit the range of morality and exempt us from agonising decisions. Take, for example, the notion of a 'conscience vote' in parliaments. The party political system will seldom countenance it, but it is arguable that most votes in parliament have a moral dimension. And it is not only decisions of government that are answerable at the bar of morality: those of state bodies that determine expenses and living-style for their functionaries are also – as are the responses of individuals to them. They affect the lives and livelihoods of a society – whoever makes them. They can be a subtle form of injustice.

We have said often enough that there is no cast-iron way of resolving moral differences. And this is particularly true, given the complexity and opaqueness of our individual lives, and the uniqueness of our relationships.

> Every single one of us is a little civilisation ... but with
> our own variant notions of what is beautiful and what
> is acceptable ... We take fortuitous resemblances
> among us to be actual likeness ... the inviolable,
> untraversable, and utterly vast spaces between us.[2]

Even the best code or tradition cannot always deal with
the particularity of your case and it is the concrete
situation that ultimately determines the morality.
Should I put my mother-in-law in a home? Should I
report my best friend for dishonesty at work? Should I
report an asylum seeker for social welfare fraud? Should
I give up my job to look after my children? Should I
leave 'an irregular union'? Should I leave the priesthood
or religious life? Should I tell my partner that I may be
HIV positive? Should I admit to the authorities that I
have been an abuser? Should I report my abusing
husband to the police? Am I able to renounce the rights
of victimhood? Some people find themselves in near-
impossible situations, some are deeply damaged, some
cope with unusually difficult urges, some are exhausted
by life's struggles. They are not all the monochrome
agents of the textbook with its arsenal of absolutes.

All that means that how we teach or train, how we
introduce morality, what understanding of it we
communicate, are delicate matters. It hardly needs
saying again that a church must welcome the emergence

2. Marilynne Robinson, *Gilead*, London, 2004, 224.

of a critical, questioning people. Not a people who languidly wait to be told what right and just living requires of them. There are so many reasons for encouraging people to make confident personal judgments – a care for the quality of their morality, an appreciation of the particular expertise which only they can bring to moral decision-making, their need to be able to deal with the particularity of their own situations. Whatever about practice, official church teaching recognises this.

> Let them [the laity] realise that their pastors will not always be so expert as to have a ready answer to every problem, even every grave problem, that arises; this is not the role of the clergy: it is rather the task of lay people to shoulder their responsibilities under the guidance of Christian wisdom and with careful attention to the teaching authority of the church.[3]

Freedom
All we can do is keep ourselves open, seek the best answer, track our prejudices and rationalisations. There is nowhere to go for answers, just as there is nowhere to go for definitive answers to issues of health or literature or the arts or history. Many people seem to believe – and perhaps it is a legacy of an all-knowing church – that it must be that we have answers to such

3. *The Church in the Modern World* 43.

matters. There may be answers, but they are too opaque for humankind. You could, as I said in the first chapter, take Aristotle's advice and consult the wise person – if you were wise enough to know who that is and to find him/her. All any adviser – friend, philosopher, priest – can do is offer their best judgment. Some might want to suggest to you what your conscience should say. But nobody can tell you what your conscience must say.

So in the end you do the best you can. You make up your mind. If you are to be true to the most sacred call of your spirit, you have to act on that. If you seriously believe that a particular course of action is right and obligatory you have no option but to follow it, and if you believe that a particular course is permissible you are entitled to follow it. How could you do anything else? How could anyone require anything else from you? To deny you this freedom of conscience is to do violence to you. It is to force you to reject what is probably your deepest human instinct, which is to honour the call of your human spirit. That is so obvious that it is hard to believe that it has taken centuries for it to be accepted. One can only think with horror of the millions who have suffered persecution, torture and death, because authorities of various hues crushed this basic light of humanity – often in the name of that cant, 'Error has no rights'. That was the deepest immorality. It still happens, of course, in spite of the lofty words about freedom in documents of church and state.

An Informed Conscience

Most people simply act regularly in accordance with character, good or bad – so that not all conscience decision is heart-rending. But we have said many times that there are difficult moments when the way of love is far from clear. We are told to consult conscience and told to act with informed conscience. What do these mean? 'Consulting' sounds like talking to oneself: are we back to thinking that conscience is a special faculty that will deliver answers to us? You hear much talk, too, of 'discerning', an honourable old term that has become something of a smoke-and-mirrors word: 'I have discerned' is sometimes slapped on the table with a finality that rejects dialogue. Consulting, discerning, can only mean allowing into consciousness what is relevant to a responsible decision. That, I grant, is a lot. It means tradition, community, faith-story, prayer. It means being sensitive to the unrepeatable features of a situation. It means an awareness of personal prejudice, of the habits of the heart which affect one's vision for good or ill.

When I have done this, I have an informed conscience. It is a much-used expression and, certainly, in the past it has been wielded as a weapon, with the strong hint that an informed conscience is one that accepts the teaching of a bishop or hierarchy, a Roman Congregation, or the Pope. It would be arrogant not to value one's tradition or to respect a teaching authority. But it is truth alone that is the binding force in matters moral. An authority can make laws but it cannot make something true. Authorities are meant to be guides who enlighten and encourage, rather than disciplinarians. They have their responsibilities for the faith of the Christian people – an unenviable task – and their firmness has at times been a bulwark for freedom and human rights. But fearlessness about the truth cuts both ways. Whether, and to what extent, detailed moral rules pertain to the core of faith is a matter of debate. Somehow, church authorities have always regarded moral conformity as crucial to the stability of their borders. Questions of faith do not appear to pose the same threats. What their people *do* seems to be more worrying.

So there has been an overwhelming temptation for authorities to pull up the drawbridge when moral issues arise and hunker down in well-worn formulae and disciplines. But the world goes on: new influences, new studies in history, anthropology, sociology and psychology, cast doubt on past teachings: the result, sadly, can be a loss of respect for authority. Nowhere has this been more obvious than in the reception accorded to *Humanae Vitae*, but it threatens now in the areas of divorce, same-sex relationships and medical research. This is not to say that popular culture, with its polls and pundits, or a counting of heads, makes things moral. But a bit of trust in the abiding presence of Christ in history, in the evolution of thought, and in the wisdom of the whole church, would not go amiss.

The weight to be given to any piece of teaching or guidance is in proportion to the likelihood of its being true guidance. That is all that conscience can be bound by. And about church teaching you have to discriminate. Everybody knows that the church authority can teach infallibly – formally by decree of the Pope or of a Council, informally by the constant and universal consent of the bishops of the world. Fortunately, it does not do so formally in moral matters, and given the restrictions that we have seen about moral rules in chapters ten and eleven, that is just as well. But it does claim that other teaching is 'authoritative', or as it was sometimes called 'authentic' – for example, papal encyclicals or decrees of the Roman congregations. This means that it should be taken seriously. But the truth of such a statement is not guaranteed in the same absolute way as the truth of an infallibly taught statement. That must be a consideration. The bottom line about such teaching – *Humanae Vitae*, sterilisation, AIH, AID, nutrition of the dying, use of 'spare' embryos for therapeutic purposes etc. – is that it can be wrong and is reformable. This does not in any sense mean that it *is* wrong.

The teaching church insists that we are to give 'a ready and respectful obedience of mind' to its statements. Is that reasonable? I think so, although one would be happier if it had the trust to consult lay people more: they have their own competence. It means that we give it the presumption of truth. Our respect for such statements of the *magisterium* derives not from some notion that an individual (the Pope) has suddenly become infallible, but from a faith that Christ will not allow his church to fall into fundamental error. It is to acknowledge that faith involves a way of life. But one is sometimes entitled to doubt: one might conclude that the way of truth does not require adherence to a particular teaching. When? It is a serious step. An individual may be a prophet – but the wise person will not jump to that conclusion. It must make a difference whether one is alone in disagreement or whether a large, committed and interested part of the Christian community, and indeed of society generally, finds a teaching defective, too rigidly stated, or too little aware of exceptional circumstances. It is not a matter of rebelliously ignoring authoritative advice. It is not a matter of 'getting away' with anything. And it is certainly not a laxness about things moral. There is a responsibility to listen to authority. But there is a truth that is deeper than authority. We need to be able to position ourselves calmly in its lambent light so that we can make the best conscience judgment in love, for ourselves and others affected by our decision.

Twenty years ago, I would have left the matter there. But things have become more complicated. It is well-known that some bishops and theologians have asked Rome to declare certain teachings to be infallibly taught, notably *Humanae Vitae*. This has not happened. But in the last few decades Rome has sought to strengthen its teaching and has inserted a category between the infallibly taught and authoritative levels which we have mentioned. It refers to this as 'definitive doctrine', teaching that is 'to be definitively held', as distinct from the authoritative, non-definitive teaching we have already considered. The usual basis for it is confirmation by the Pope that certain teachings have always been held by the universal body of bishops, the ordinary and universal *magisterium*. Examples are the statement of the Pontifical Council for the Family that 'The Church has always taught the intrinsic evil of contraception ... This teaching is to be held as definitive and irreformable.'[4] Likewise, condemnations of abortion, direct killing of the innocent, and euthanasia in *Evangelium Vitae*, and of homosexual acts. While it has not declared these teachings to be infallibly taught, the intention obviously is to give them considerable binding-force, something just short of infallible. A particularly striking example was the declaration that women could not be ordained priests (*Ordinatio Sacerdotalis*, 1994), something that was later declared by a Roman congregation (itself not infallible!) to be infallible.

Many theologians find great technical problems about the nature of this teaching: a discussion of that would take me too far afield here. And also about the possibility of establishing, in individual instances, that the bishops of the world have always, and do now, positively agree that something is to be held definitively

4. *Morality of Conjugal Life*, 16.

and irrevocably.[5] But where does it leave conscience? One will recognise that the new language seeks to impress on us the seriousness of the matter in question and one will certainly take that into account. But is hard to see that a demand of this kind – 'to be held definitively' – which does not carry with it the assurance of infallibility, can ask any more of the individual conscience than the serious and respectful consideration that we have already required for authentic/authoritative teaching.

Conscience and Emotions: Guilt

Conscience is experienced as a matter of feeling, very often as a matter of guilt. That is only to be expected. We have noted how intimately emotions suffuse moral life. It is not surprising that the experience of conscience is surrounded by feelings. We say that conscience troubles us or that we feel guilt or know remorse: we talk about 'the worm of conscience' – just as we can speak of the peace or joy of a good conscience. That witnesses to the elemental depth of the moral dimension. What is important is that guilt be appropriate. I have mentioned the pseudo-conscience of the super-ego, which confuses us with niggling fears and guilt. True guilt is cleaner. It is not about fear but about a sense of

5. The interested reader could pursue this in Francis A. Sullivan, *Creative Fidelity: Weighing and Interpreting Documents of the Magisterium*, Eugene, Oregon, 2003, or Richard R. Gaillardetz, *Teaching with Authority: A Theology of the Magisterium in the Church*, Collegeville, 1997.

having been untrue to one's self. True remorse is not just emotional, not just an unfortunate psychic kink. It is, you might say, metaphysical: it is constitutive of one's being, a reaction of one's soul. The world could do with a great deal more of it. Today, deep moral failure, behaviour destructive of the life and hopes of whole communities, is easily trivialised. But there is the other side of the story, too – the utterly excessive and misguided guilt that has ravaged the lives of generations of Catholics. Few things would make you more sceptical of the role of religion.

A different kind of danger is the triumph of the therapeutic. We run to psychotherapists to ease the pain of guilt. Is it that we assume that we are due a life of easy, sunny happiness, unclouded by jagged reminders of our deviousness, dishonesty, or grossness? We can be persuaded that our unease is pathological, arising only out of unfortunate inner fears, badly needing to be airbrushed from our consciousness. True, guilt may be unwarranted and in need of being psychologically resolved. True, we need to be understanding and patient of our failures and those of others. The mistake, however, is always to insist that our unease points to no real wrong, that it has no moral message for us. That artificially removes the challenge and the pain, which are inseparable from human life. Morality is not an illusion. It is intrinsic to the human condition. It sometimes makes uncomfortable demands. We cannot deny it without stifling our spirit.

Postscript

Let me try to pull some of this together. The issue for us is what to make of our moral lives. I am especially interested in how we situate morality in our lives and with what notion of it we work. They are questions that often lie unexamined but that greatly affect us.

Christianity is essentially a religious faith. It is not just a moral system or tradition. We distinguish faith from belief, although we often use them inter-changeably. In a religious context we normally think of belief as a trusting willingness to give intellectual assent to certain truths proposed to us. So – do you believe in an afterlife, or do you believe that Jesus rose from the dead? Faith is more dynamic. It is a deep kind of trust that involves commitment. It crops up continually in the gospels, as it did in the Old Testament. Here faith is an active committed trust of a very comprehensive kind in God's gift of self. It is about trusting enough to give one's heart and soul, a trust that is a choice about the very meaning of our existence. And that is necessarily trust about a lot of related things – about the source of our life, about the nature of it, about its end-point, about our destiny, about right living, about the significance of desire and hope and love, about how we ought, not only to think about, but to feel about ourselves and others, about the fate of the world. To have faith in Jesus Christ is to trust him in this radical way. Faith and morality are to be distinguished but faith gives morality its overall context.

Much of what we know about Jesus, we know as in a mirror, in the accounts we have of the experience of those who gathered around him in faith, who tried to catch his spirit, to pass on his sayings. We find it in our scriptures in a great variety of ways. It is easy to make facile assumptions, to jump to conclusions about who Jesus was and what he saw as his mission. We are continually learning more about that: we have new knowledge about his time and place and traditions. From age to age, we are confronted with the question: who is Jesus for us?; or, one might ask, which Jesus? Because different images of Jesus have emerged. But we have a fair picture in the New Testament and in our traditions. What is undeniable is that his basic message was one of the prodigal care and love of God for humankind, of God's design for the healing, well-being and wholeness of all peoples. What he preached, and what his presence signified, was God's continuing covenant or commitment to his people, the inauguration of the reign of God and his desire for its ultimate realisation. That means liberation from deprivation of various kinds – from Godlessness, from loneliness, from meaninglessness, from oppression, from marginalisation, from poverty, from sinfulness – to fullness and wholeness of life. You may not like the image of Christ the King but one thing the feast did was to give us a very striking Preface of the Mass, which hopes for 'a kingdom of truth and life, a kingdom of holiness and grace, a kingdom of justice, love, and peace'. That might be the church's summary of the thrust of Christ's mission.

That, of course, is a million miles away from what we have now. It remains a dream but also a task for those who follow Christ, who share faith in him. A dream, especially, because he appeared to be particularly and counter-culturally concerned about those who were in most need of liberation and lifting-up – the poor, the marginalised, the despised, the neglected. It is they who have most reason to look forward to, and who know best, what the reign of God might mean. Unless we listen to them, we have only a very thin notion of what gospel hope and salvation mean. You could say that the test of the community of Christ today is the extent to which it shows something of his care – whether it has allowed the love of God to be poured into our hearts for the flourishing of others, whether it has the bias of Jesus towards the most needy.

A key concern for me in the book was to say that this religious message takes up, promotes and enhances the most fundamental of human insights. That is, insight about the preciousness of human beings created by God. They are, each one, every one, everywhere, at all times, whatever they think or feel or do, whatever their talents or lack of talent, worthy of respect. In themselves, for themselves. This recognition of the created person, the demand which this makes on us, is what I mean when I talk about the autonomy of morality. If we do not acknowledge the inherent value of every other we do not do justice to God's creation. The whole Christ story gives this primacy, situates it in the creative act of God's love, and in the final promise of destiny with God. Faith-engagement with Christ is meant to draw us all into that elemental respect and love. We are in the image of God, sharers of the divine nature. Our lives are to be an identification with Christ – 'I live now, not I, but Christ lives in me' – a transformation of our hearts into the desires and values of his heart – not a cold and grudging submission to law. So that, in our own limited and faltering way, we, too, will bring about God's reign. There will be no 'kingdom of justice, love and peace' unless we become agents of justice, love and peace. God loves others through us. God loves us through others.

As I see it, then, Christ points to our possibilities and our responsibilities. He is the way and it is instructive that his early followers referred to Christian life as The Way. Not surprisingly, even in the very early days, there was difference and conflict among them about what that entailed, some of it honest, some perverse. What is important for our purposes is how the moral strand developed – what we inherited and where we are with it now. Behaviour came to be crucial in the scheme of things: a style of life was what identified the community. But rather than opening to the broad expanse of God's purposes for human wholeness, it came in time to be tied into the demands for personal salvation. 'What must I do to inherit eternal life': 'keep the commandments'. This was what prevailed. Theologians are fond of saying that the problem about Christian morality is that it came to be divorced from the great thrust of Christian truths – systematic theology – and acquired a life of its own. That is true, but only partly so. In fact, it came to be lodged in certain elements of the story – that God creates us, that he has given us commandments, that we can merit eternal life if we behave well, that this is the one thing necessary, that we will be judged on our behaviour. That was a selective interpretation, a particular and inadequate model of God's dealings with us, which emerged and which prevailed until relatively recent times. That was the context in which Christians lived their lives.

The complaint of some authors in the last century that moral theology had become a science of sin may not have been far off the mark. Since one's personal salvation was the key concern, sin and failure dominated life. And since the only hope after shipwreck was the sacrament of Penance, there grew up an intense discipline about confessional practice, about the possibility of forgiveness, about conditions for absolution, about the role of the confessor. It is well-known that the moral teaching which priests received, especially after the Council of Trent, was almost entirely about confession, about the number and kinds of sin, about the need for repentance, about true sorrow. Much of it was highly rigorist. It is depressing to read the manuals of the nineteenth and early twentieth centuries, their severe teaching on habits and occasions of sin, their warnings to confessors that, as judges, they were to be particularly careful about granting absolution.[1] Even if pastoral practice was more benign than the textbook, even if there was some recognition that sins of weakness are less grave than sins of malice, one has to recognise sadly that there developed a toxic cocktail of control, discipline and fear. This was no ordinary judge, and no ordinary fear about

---

1. The interested reader could consult Raphael Gallagher, 'The Fate of the Moral Manual since Saint Alphonsus', in Enda McDonagh and Vincent MacNamara (eds), *An Irish Reader in Moral Theology: The Legacy of the Last Fifty Years*, Dublin, 2009. He says of the influential author, Antoine, whose work went into sixty editions in the eighteenth and nineteenth centuries, 'One senses that the main concern is with the confessor as controller of the confessional tribunal ... the overall tone is of the great difficulty in granting absolution ... a begrudging attitude even towards those who are contrite ... [which] contributed to despair among ordinary people and, in time, to the great pastoral problem of the neglect of the sacraments'. 62–3.

some inner-worldly calamity. It was fear for one's eternal happiness or suffering: the confessor seemed to hold your final destiny in his hands. And so, the anger today of those who felt individually humiliated, and of those who feel that the church-inspired laws and prejudices of society crippled their freedom. It is not the whole story, of course: there was in church life beauty, and wisdom, and virtue, and imagination, and outreaches of care and concern. But it is a sad part of it.

I always feel a bit guilty when dwelling on failures of the past. There is nothing as tiresome as someone taking easy pot-shots. As in many other areas of life, one has at times to acknowledge that a practice or teaching was misguided but, at the same time, understandable. We know our own limitations. We are all locked into our cultures and limited by our horizons: it often seems unthinkable to question them. And, I suppose, dangerous. Happily, things have changed. Certainly, horrific revelations have made for a chastened and humbler church. But it is not only that. From within the church itself a richer, kindlier life has emerged. It has listened to the call to renew itself. It has reached into its wisdom. It may be that Vatican II is as distant from most young people as Trent or Chalcedon. They have never known the fear or abasement of their elders. But the religious climate in which they live owes much to that Council. One of the features that has largely disappeared is the very model that dominated for so long and that blighted the lives of older generations. The notion of an apparently grudging God, who demands an almost impossible uprightness, whose love has to be earned the hard way, has been turned on its head by many authors, and by Christians generally in their new-found freedom and courage. Their starting-point is the loving-kindness and mercy of God: in that we trust. One Irish theologian has put it neatly: we have moved from 'if X then Y' – if you earn God's love by constant vigilance you will receive it – to 'Y therefore X' – God loves you first, as the Epistle of John insists, therefore be inspired by that love.[2] There is much more of that today. There is renewal. Morality is better placed now within a broader theology. For all the frightening abuses which have emerged in church practice, perhaps theology is inching, in John McGahern's words, from a fortress church of edicts, threats and punishments to a church of spires and brilliant windows that go towards love and light.

But we have learned from other sources, too. What is the human heart no one knows better than the creator God. What our flourishing will mean, what our true evolution, is known only to him/her. But we here have to go on searching to know the human project, to understand what are the great dynamics of our lives, and what our possibilities. We have to engage with the sciences. Think of what anthropology and evolutionary theory tell us about origins. Think of what cosmology

2. Eamonn Bredin, *Disturbing the Peace: The Way of Disciples*, Dublin, 1985, 123ff.

tells us about the far-offness of creation, of our direct descent from the Big Bang and the first stirrings of life, of the manner in which we are all – sun and stars, fire and water and light and rock and insect and plant and animal – intimately related in a cosmic whole. We are one family. Think of what psychology and neuroscience tell us about the psycho-dynamic emergence of the personality, about the significance of our unconscious life: the explosion of knowledge in the last hundred years or so has shed light on dark caverns of our psyche and has revolutionised our understanding of ourselves. Think of how the spiritual traditions, most recently those of the East, have introduced us to new vistas of the human spirit. Think of what social theory and theories of language have told us of how we perceive people, cultures, situations, obligations – the presuppositions that often lead us astray. Think poetry and art and drama.

They tell us whom God created, *who we are*. What is important for our purposes here is that they tell much about the moral agent, the one who is to serve the reign of God. We cannot know what we are at unless we are in touch with this thinking, and we are only beginning to glimpse what this will mean for moral life. I have only been able to gesture towards it. It is all in God's providence for us. It fills out ideas of the covenant of the creator-God with us, and of the mission of Christ. We have come, in God's providence, through the long evolutionary process with its strange and winding ways. We are born with a bewildering concoction of needs and

hopes and fears. It is comforting that the first followers
of Jesus assure us that he appealed not only to our sense
of beauty and wonder and love, but recognised our
confusion and ambivalence, our likelihood to be blown
off course in the high wind of life. He recognised that
the strange mixture, which each of us is, would call for
long patience not only with others but with ourselves.

Throughout the book I have suggested that all this
might make us look more understandingly at the human
condition, at the mysterious unfurling of each one's life,
at how time and place and happening have affected the
moral capacity of each of us, often through no fault of
our own. One would hope that, in its moral teaching and
discipline, a more patient church might be more sensitive
to difference, more tentative in judgment, more wary of
absolutes, more ready to honour individuality. The
central mission for us is to be mediators of the loving-
kindness and mercy of God. That – and all that goes with
it – is our worldly task. What is most crucial for us is the
hoped-for transformation which in some fashion will
align our minds and hearts with that. But it seems
important to say that, with all that, we have to be aware
of the constraints of the human condition – aware of
what we can say about morality, or hope to accomplish,
or expect from others. Christian vision does not
magically resolve problems or absolve us from the
patient search for moral truth and understanding.

Talk of God's love could be idealistic, romantic,
depressing: we are so conscious of how far we are

removed from it. But we must allow the conviction of it to continue to give hope to ourselves and our world: faith in that love is the deepest down truth of our religious culture. If his presence to us is a visitation of mercy, we can calmly accept our own woundedness and learn to live with our failures. We have to. It is the human condition. Failure is one of humankind's most pervasive myths. We have to own the wayward elements in our own and in human nature, and yet to hope. Let us not forget that we all have known also our moments of glad grace. I would bet that we have been astonished just as much by the goodness, the sacrifice, the commitment, that we often find around us, as by the crookedness and venality. The love that courses in the veins of human life is as great a mystery as the evil. Most fundamentally, what we are more confident about is that our lives are meant to be lived in a context of trust, in which our moral success or failure is not the last word. We live and move and have our being within a Presence who broods over the long evolution of our race, who knows that we carry the human stain, the elemental wound of human nature, who appreciates the curve of each personal history. Who is more sensitive to the complexity of our lives than any human legislator, even those who purport to represent him/her. Who does not judge as we judge. Who has told us to trust more in God's loving-kindness than in the righteousness of our doings. Who understands failure. We can only be patient.